Ch'ang Hon Taekwon-Do Hosinsul
Self Defence Techniques
From Ch'ang Hon (ITF) Taekwon-Do

CheckPoint
Press

Ch'ang Hon Taekwon-Do Hosinsul
Self Defence Techniques
From Ch'ang Hon (ITF) Taekwon-Do

Warning

This book contains dangerous techniques which can result in serious injury or death. Neither the author nor publisher can accept any responsibility for any prosecution or proceedings brought or instituted against any person or body as a result of the use or misuse of information or techniques described or detailed within this book or any injury, loss or damage caused thereby. The techniques and training methods described in this book require high levels of skill, control and fitness and should only be practiced by those in good health and under the supervision of a qualified instructor.

Ch'ang Hon Taekwon-Do Hosinsul
Self Defence Techniques
From Ch'ang Hon (ITF) Taekwon-Do

By Stuart Anslow

Photographs by Kate Barry & Trupz Mahida
Cover Design by Liam Cullen
Interior Layout by Stuart Anslow
Edited by John Dowding

British Library Cataloguing In Publication Data
A Record of this Publication is available
from the British Library

ISBN 978-1-906628-74-1

Published by
CheckPoint Press, Ireland,
www.checkpointpress.com

This book is dedicated to Steve Cacchia

1962 to 2016

"The song is ended but the melody lingers on…"
—Irving Berlin

"A student said to his master: "You teach me fighting, but you talk about peace. How do you reconcile the two?" The master replied: "It is better to be a warrior in a garden than to be a gardener in a war."

Acknowledgements

If you face just one opponent but doubt yourself, you are outnumbered

No martial artist could put a book together without help, help which started a long time before I set pen to paper or before I even considered writing this book, help from my own instructors, Master David Bryan and Mr John Pepper, from the day I started Taekwon-Do, help from those I trained with, those I have trained under, those I have crossed paths with along my journey, in fact everyone who has added to my knowledge of martial arts which has culminated in this book., I thank you all.

Of course, there are those who in one way of another have indirectly helped me with this book and there are those who have helped me directly. So I wish to thank my proof reader John Dowding for not only correcting my fast finger typing errors, but also casting his critical eye over my work, offering advice on how things comes across and the many laughs we have whilst doing it all, which makes the most tedious part of writing a book wholly more enjoyable. I would like to thank my students Kate Barry and Trupz Mahida who gave up some of their precious training time to take the many photographs that appear in this book, as well as thanking all those who have appeared in the photographs as well, some taking on bumps and bruises along the way, to ensure the photographs are as good as possible. These were a mix of my own students; Vikram Gautam, Elaine Cacchia, Lyndsey Reynolds, Suliman Majeed, Parvez Sultan, Umar Marikar, Matt Baxter, Maciek and Helen Krychowski, Tomasz Ostrowski, Trupz Mahida, Maiya Radia, Chetan Patel, Vesa Kelani, Kirtan Amin, Saeed Yusufi, Zynab Zakaria and Chris Corcoran; as well as some from schools of fellow Instructors and friends of mine; Hay Harris and his students Martin Addy and Steve Kennedy, Shane Heslin (a student of Master Doug Cook's Chosun Taekwondo Academy in New York) and Steve Cacchia (a student of Master Andrew Rhee in Australia) and husband of my (and Master Rhee's student), Elaine. Steve sadly passed away whilst finalising this book.

And whilst maybe you 'should never judge a book by its cover', a great cover does go a long way, so I thank my friend Liam Cullen for once again designing the awesome cover for this book, which I feel is a great representation of its content.

I would also like to thank you, the reader, whether student or instructor (or likely both), not only for getting this book, but for looking to increase your knowledge and perhaps teachings and thus helping keep Taekwon-Do alive as the martial art it should be.

"Only a warrior chooses pacifism;
others are condemned to it."

About The Author

There is no comfort in the growth zone and no growth in the comfort zone

Stuart Anslow started Taekwon-Do formally in early 1991, receiving his black belt in March, 1994. And at the time of writing has been studying Taekwon-Do continuously, without a break, for over 25 years, with close to 30 years in martial arts altogether.

He is Chief Instructor of the renowned Rayners Lane Taekwon-Do Academy, which was established in April 1999 and is based in London, UK.

During his martial arts career, Stuart has won many accolades in the sporting arena, including national and world titles. His Academy has been very successful in competition, winning many gold medals at every martial arts championship his students enter, a testament to his abilities as an instructor. To date he has produced 11 World Gold medallist students and is the Taekwon-Do instructor of movie star Dev Patel from *'Slumdog Millionaire'*, whom he trained from white to black belt.

In 2000, Stuart won a gold and silver medal at Grandmaster Hee, Il Cho's 1st AIMAA Open World Championships and in 2004 he returned with 14 of his students to the 2nd AIMAA Open World Championships where they brought home 26 medals between them, 7 of them becoming World Champions in their own right, 2 became double world gold medallists, all from a single school of Taekwon-Do. In 2012 he took 13 students to the PUMA World Opens and collectively his students won 28 medals, 6 of which were gold's, with one student again becoming a double world gold medallist.

Receiving a medal at the 2000 World Championships, from Grandmaster Hee Il Cho

In 2002, Stuart founded the International Alliance of Martial Arts Schools (IAOMAS) which drew martial artists from around the world together, growing

from a few schools to over 400 in under a year. This non-profit organization is an online student and instructor support group that gives travelling students the ability to train at hundreds of affiliated schools worldwide and is truly unique in the way it operates and is still running with the same model today.

Stuart has been a regular writer for the UK martial arts press, having written many articles for *'Taekwon-Do and Korean Martial Arts'*, *'Combat'*, *'Martial Arts Illustrated'* and *'Fighters'* magazines, as well as taking part in interviews for some of them. He now mainly writes for *'Totally Tae Kwon Do'* magazine. His numerous articles[1] cover the many related subjects of martial arts from training to motivation, but his main love is Taekwon-Do. As well as his Academy, Stuart is the Chief martial arts instructor for a private school, which was one of the first schools in the country to teach martial arts as part of its national curriculum.

In 2002, Stuart received an award from the Hikaru Ryu Dojo, a martial arts academy in Australia, presented by their Chief Instructor and fellow IAOMAS member Colin Wee when he visited Stuart's Academy in the UK. In recognizing Stuart's contribution, Colin stated (referring to IAOMAS) that *"nothing to date has been so foresighted and effective as Stuart's work in establishing this worldwide online martial arts community."* Colin now runs IAOMAS.[2]

Receiving a his award from Sabum-nim Colin Wee in 2002

Combat magazines 'Hall Of Fame' award, 2003

In October 2003, Stuart was inducted into the world renowned Combat Magazine *'Hall Of Fame 2003'* for his work within the field of martial arts on a worldwide level. Combat magazine was the UK and Europe's biggest martial arts publication.

In 2004 he was selected as the Assistant Coach for the Harrow Borough Karate Squad, to compete at the prestigious London Youth Games held at Crystal Palace each year. This position he held for 5 years before having to give it up due to time constraints with his work in Taekwon-Do. During the same year Stuart also received various Honorary awards for his work in the international field of martial arts. From the USA he received a *'Yap Suk Dai Ji Discipleship'* award for his innovative work within IAOMAS and *'T'ang Shou'* society award for promoting martial arts on a worldwide scale.

In 2006 he was presented with a *'Certificate Of Appreciation'* from the members of

---

[1] Many of the articles can be found by visiting www.raynerslanetkd.com and www.harrowtkd.com, the Academy website's
[2] See www.iaomas.com

IAOMAS Canada which read '*In recognition of your undying contribution to the evolution of martial arts and your inspirational and innovative formation of the International Alliance Of Martial Art Schools*'.

Also in 2006 he released his first book relating to Taekwon-do; '*Ch'ang Hon Taekwon-do Hae Sul: Real Applications To The ITF Patterns Vol: 1*' which explored the applications of patterns techniques contained within the Ch'ang Hon patterns, away from what was considered the '*norm*' for applications in favour of more realistic (and ultimately more beneficial) techniques. The book was extremely well received and became an instant success, seen as a 'must have' by both instructors and students worldwide.

In 2009, his love for Taekwon-Do and disappointment with the coverage in the various Taekwon-Do magazines led him to publish his own online magazine '*Totally Tae Kwon Do*'; which was a magazine for all students of the art, irrespective of system or style. Supported by his friends, Tae Kwon Do instructors and students around the world it too became a worldwide success.

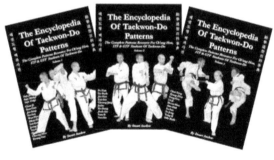

In 2010 he released 3 more books titled '*The Encyclopedia Of Taekwon-Do Patterns:: The Complete Pattern Resource For Ch'ang Hon, ITF & GTF Students Of Taekwon-Do*' which featured all 25 of General Choi's patterns, as well as those of Grandmaster Park Jung Tae and the knife pattern by Grandmaster Kim Bok Man, plus the 3 saju exercises - a feat that had never been published before. All were extensively detailed in a way that had never been done before either, setting the template for how future books on patterns and kata should be done. These books received worldwide acclaim as well.

Also in 2010 Stuart received a 'Citation of Appreciation', signed by Dr. Choue Chung-won, President of the World Taekwondo Federation, which reads: '*In recognition of your dedicated service and outstanding contribution to the development of Taekwondo*'

Citation of Appreciation, signed by Dr. Choue, President of the WTF

In 2012 he released the much anticipated 2nd volume of *'Ch'ang Hon Taekwon-do Hae Sul: Real Applications To The ITF Patterns'* which followed on where Vol. 1 had left off, exploring realistic applications for the patterns from 2nd Kup to 2nd Degree.

In 2013 he released a book on the in-depth histories behind the Taekwon-Do patterns of his system, titled *'From Creation To Unification: The Complete Histories behind The Ch'ang Hon (ITF) Patterns'* which again, was extremely well received worldwide.

Stuart has taught in the USA and other countries and in 2015 toured South Korea and taught Taekwon-Do in its homeland, at various historical locations around the country.

In 2016 Stuart, along with Dr. George Vitale and Totally Tae Kwon Do magazine played a pivotal role in achieving recognition for General Choi Hong Hi at the Taekwondowon's *'Hall of Greats'*, in Muju, South Korea. He also took part in the *'Worlds Largest Taekwon-Do Display'* making him a Guinness World Record holder as well.

Stuart is well known in the UK and internationally and apart from being a full time instructor of Taekwon-do, running local Self Protection courses, national seminars, writing and publishing books on the art of Taekwon-Do as well as publishing the monthly *Totally Tae Kwon Do* magazine, he is the father of four beautiful children, whom he supports and cherishes. His work in Taekwon-Do, both through his teaching of the art as well as his articles and books, is not only held in high regards by those who practice the Ch'ang Hon (ITF) system, but also respected by many in the WTF (World Taekwondo Federation) as well as students of other martial arts.

Stuarts reputation is gained not only by his own career but also by his uncompromising approach to teaching, the standards within his Academy and that of his students and his views of not watering down the martial art of Taekwon-Do. His students quality are testament of his *'no short cuts'* approach to how martial arts in general and Taekwon-Do in particular, should be taught. His classes flourish with quality students despite much competition from schools with a more *relaxed* approach to teaching, requirements and gradings and he continues to help take Taekwon-Do into the future as a fully rounded martial art.

Table Of Contents

Table Of Contents

Introduction

Many students take up Taekwon-Do (or any martial art for that matter) specifically in order to learn how to defend themselves should they ever be attacked for real; and whilst training in a martial art offers lots of additional benefits (fitness, competitions, socialisation etc.), for many this is their number one motivation for stepping into the dojang.

Whilst all parts of training offer some attributes relating to self-defence, for most schools, this area is addressed specifically during the practice of Hosinsul.

Whilst not all schools practice Hosinsul, for those that do, there are certain issues that arise. For General Choi Hong Hi, Hosinsul was seen as a higher level of practice, that followed on from basics, patterns, free sparring and conditioning work, however, whilst this sounds nice in theory, it is a rather romantic notion in my opinion, mainly due to the way certain sections of the art are practiced - meaning there is a big disconnect between the major areas of the art, such as patterns and sparring and these do not easily 'connect' with practicing Hosinsul. For example, many schools only practice patterns for 'performance', so they can be used to pass gradings or win medals at competitions. Consequently free sparring is practiced in a 'competition' format only, meaning it actually uses a very limited number of techniques, as opposed to General Choi's description of free sparring seeing the use of *'all available means and methods'*[3]. Due to this, instructors are not able to 'connect the dots' and often seek outside influences, such as Hapkido or Krav Maga to fill the void in their schools Hosinsul.

Schools that do not practice Hosinsul may not do so for a number of reasons, maybe they wish to focus on the sport element of the art, maybe they do not even realise it is an instrumental part of Taekwon-Do or maybe they simply do not know how to implement it properly, as the instructors are not versed in realistic self defence techniques themselves!

This book has a dual purpose; firstly it is designed to help instructors incorporate a Hosinsul section into their classes, thus addressing the students need for self defence training.

Secondly, its purpose is to give students and instructors ideas for defence techniques that actually come directly from Taekwon-Do itself, negating the need to turn to other arts to fill the void, in turn helping to push Taekwon-Do forward as a more complete art in itself, making what you teach or practice closer to the art General Choi envisaged.

---

[3] Quoted from the 15 Volume Encyclopedia of Taekwon-Do by General Choi Hong Hi; Chapter 5 - Free Sparring

With that said, this book is not 'all encompassing'; it offers ideas for you to explore within your Hosinsul practice sessions, as when it comes to self defence the most important aspect of it is that what you are actually practicing, will work for you, the student, for real, should you ever have to use it.

Of course, it is well known that the more repetition you have in your training, the better a technique will work for you when you need it, which is why I have endeavoured to bring quite a few techniques and combinations directly from the patterns of Taekwon-Do, to show how they can be used for self defence, as well as using fundamental movements and other areas of training such as the throws of Taekwon-Do.

*"Give me 6 hours to chop down a tree
and I will spend the first 4 sharpening my axe"*

- *Abraham Lincoln*

Chapter 1
The Practice Of Hosinsul

What is Hosinsul?

On a basic level, Hosinsul simply means 'self defence techniques' and for the student of Taekwon-Do, it is the practice of self defence.

호신술 – The term Hosinsul is actually three words linked together, Ho, Sin and Sul and when translated literally (from Hangul), 'Ho' translates as 'protection', 'Sin' translates as 'body' and 'Sul' translates as 'technique', so combined they mean 'techniques to protect the body'[4], in other words 'self defence'.

In his 15 volume encyclopedia General Choi wrote the Romanized version as 'Hosin Sul'. However, the more modern version should be written as a single word, with the pronunciation (and spelling) being 'Hoshinsul'.[4] However, I have kept closer to the way General Choi spelt it for the purpose of this book, as that's how most Ch'ang Hon (ITF) students and instructors would recognise it.

In the dojang Hosinsul is often a separate form of practice and training for more senior grades, however, if you look at Taekwon-Do more closely, whilst Hosinsul is often practiced as a separate section of a class, it actually overlaps with the practice of Patterns, 1 Step Sparring and Free Sparring.

The whole idea of Hosinsul practice is to teach and prepare students to defend themselves against realistic attacks in real life situations and thus, is a vital element of study and practice in any Taekwon-Do school.

Students practicing Hosinsul in class

---

[4] Translation courtesy of Taekwondo Instructor and author, Sabum-nim Jeff Rosser.

Hosinsul In Taekwon-Do

When General Choi was putting together the various elements that were to make Taekwon-Do complete, he sought what he considered *'advanced techniques*[5] to cover the Hosinsul area of Taekwon-Do and detailed them as a separate section within his manuals.

While obviously this was a good idea, its implementation wasn't ideal, as like other parts of the art, it was kept segregated, as an isolated section. Ideally it should of overlapped other areas of the art, but just as patterns remained a practice in isolation, with hardly any over-lap into the type of Free Sparring performed in Taekwon-Do, the Hosinsul element didn't draw fully from other areas of the art either.

In order to develop and show some effective self defence techniques in his manual, apart from the basic blocks, kicks and strikes of Taekwon-Do, General Choi sought the help of instructors that as well as Taekwon-Do, also held black belts in other arts; specifically for Hosinsul these were Yudo (Judo) and Hapkido.

In his manuals you will see a whole section on throwing and falling techniques, something that is rarely practiced in many Taekwon-do schools, but is an important element in regards to Taekwon-Do Hosinsul. In the Hosinsul section you will also see some of the locks and manipulations from Hapkido, though General Choi was very specific about what he wanted and what he didn't want within the Hosinsul element of Taekwon-Do, which meant he kept some of the basic techniques but didn't want the more 'flowery' techniques that you often see in Hapkido.

As the art developed and it gathered a worldwide following, much attention was placed on the performance of patterns and executing them in the specific way that General Choi wanted, with little to no thought about the practical side of them - as self defence techniques - though by definition they still remained *'attack or defence techniques, set to a fixed and logical sequence*[6]. Other misunderstandings or misconceptions about patterns, blocks and other attributes associated with them has led to the decline in patterns being used for realistic Hosinsul altogether.

The rise of competition has led to the decline of Hosinsul practice within the dojang, with instructors drilling their students in 'correct' competition pattern performance, as well as sport style sparring and all that's associated with it, leaving little time for Hosinsul practice, if indeed it is practiced at all.

However, if you follow the 'Cycle of Taekwon-Do' that General Choi produced,

---

[5] Encyclopedia of Taekwon-Do by General Choi Hong Hi; Chapter 5 - Self-Defence Techniques (Hosin Sul)

[6] Encyclopedia of Taekwon-Do by General Choi Hong Hi; Chapter 8 - Patterns (Tul)

you will see that whilst the training of Taekwon-Do starts with the basics (fundamental movements), then patterns, then sparring, then 'dallyon' (conditioning of the body), the last part of the cycle, where everything has been leading to, is Hosinsul.

So it is clear that General Choi felt that Hosinsul, while advanced, was a vital element of Taekwon-do and thus an important element to practice regularly.

However, if your dojang doesn't practice Hosinsul, the very concept of it is difficult to put into practice. For example, the attacking student will lack

The Cycle of Taekwon-Do

idea's of what constitutes a 'realistic' attack and thus attack with techniques like standard obverse punches or high section reverse turning kicks, which whilst undoubtedly Taekwon-Do techniques, are unlikely to be used by a non-Taekwon-Do trained aggressor.

Consequently, students draw from their 'Step Sparring' and 'Free Sparring' skills for their defences, which for the most part are performed at medium to long range, whereas most common street attacks happen at close range, leaving the student ill-prepared for such assaults.

This lack of close range skills has forced instructors to seek out knowledge from other arts to cover this perceived 'gap' in Taekwon-Do and thus resort to simply replacing the whole of Hosinsul practice with a Hapkido section or going to arts like Krav Maga for inspiration and practical techniques, which takes us further away from Taekwon-Do being a complete art.

Whilst using other arts may seem like the solution, if you study Taekwon-Do in-depth, you will see that its not really necessary. It may even seem contradictory, seeing as General Choi already utilised techniques from other arts, but the point is, due to General Choi's foresight in trying to attain realistic techniques for self defence by 'borrowing' from other arts, they are already infused in Taekwon-Do and over time became Taekwon-Do anyway.

With that said, utilising techniques from other arts isn't wrong either. In my dojang I often tell my students that the most important thing in Hosinsul is that it works and if what you know so far, within Taekwon-Do isn't sufficient, then by all means use something you get from elsewhere, as at the end of the day, when your life is on the line, no one is going to care that the technique that saved you came from Taekwon-Do, Krav Maga, Hapkido or Thai-Boxing.

What will matter is you finding out that the techniques you thought would work... don't! And that will be a tough lesson to learn... if you survive it!

That's why it's important to make your Hosinsul as realistic as possible and to do that we need to train as realistically as possible, with both realistic attacks and defences, performed in a realistic manner via various training methods, coupled with some other aspects such as contact and intent.

To train Hosinsul realistically we need to have the following elements:

1. *Realistic attacks to defend against* - we find these not in Taekwon-Do, but from studies such as the HAOV[7] (Habitual Acts of Violence) list and other sources.

2. *Realistic defences* - we can find these both within Taekwon-Do (fundamentals and patterns) and elsewhere.

3. *Realistic practice methods*

The Bigger Picture

Whilst one of the aims of this book is to give you some ideas for your Hosinsul practice, it's just one part of the spectrum of good self defence.

The term 'self defence' is really a catch all term, that actually covers more than just the techniques to defend yourself. On either side of Hosinsul we have both *self-protection* and *fighting* and all 3 elements overlap each other.

Self-Protection is the practice of avoiding and assessing potential trouble in the first place, it includes such areas as situational awareness, target hardening (making yourself less of a target to aggressors), colour codes (your state of readiness) and many other, non-physical elements. Some good old 'common sense' doesn't hurt either!

Fighting is exactly that, we may call the training of it 'sparring' in the dojang, but it is not to be confused with competition style free sparring, although elements of competition free-sparring can of course be helpful to real fighting. In my dojang we differentiate between the two by calling the 'realistic' fighting side 'Traditional

---

[7] HAOV is a list compiled by martial arts instructor, researcher and author Sensei Patrick McCarthy a few years ago (but in modern times) and is a list of the most common street attacks.

Sparring' so students know exactly what they are getting into when we do it. Traditional Sparring allows everything that competition sparring does, as well as low kicks, sweeps, throws, locks, takedowns etc. (within safety limits) and helps the students learn what does and doesn't work in a real fight situation.

In theory, if you employ good solid self protection principles properly, you will never have to use what you practice in Hosinsul. However, no one is 100% perfect and sometimes things just happen, so when self protection goes wrong, we have Hosinsul, to deal with the situation. But if what we do in hosinsul goes wrong, then we have no choice but to fight.

In short:

- Good self protection skills stops you getting into trouble in the first place.
- Good Hosinsul deals with trouble at the onset, before we have to fight.
- If it all goes wrong and we have to fight, we want to have given ourselves the best chance possible to win through and be victorious.

On top of all that, knowledge of the law in your own country (or any you travel to) is a good idea, knowing what constitutes 'reasonable force' as well as how to deal with the Police and the authorities.

The knowledge of how your body acts under stress (adrenaline surges, 'fight or flight', flinch response and other natural reactions) is also important to understand.

Understanding how the human body works is of course very useful, it doesn't have to be in-depth, you don't have to know every pressure point ever listed, just some basics like a straight arm equals a weak elbow, but a bent one means its strong, vital points (eyes, floating ribs, side of the knee and so on), the effects you get by striking certain area's or twisting certain parts (such as the head), much of which you will learn by reading this book.

The Difference Between 1 Step Sparring and Hosinsul

Both 1 Step Sparring and Hosinsul are elements of Taekwon-Do practice and whilst virtually all students practice 1 Step Sparring, surprisingly many do not practice Hosinsul and when they do, they often confuse the two or see them as the same thing.

When I took my 3rd degree grading, we had just completed some Free Sparring and previous to that we performed 1 Step Sparring. After the Free Sparring, the Chief Examiner paired us up and told us to perform Hosinsul. Unfortunately, the person

Chapter 1:
The Practice of Hosinsul

I was paired with didn't have a clue what Hosinsul entailed, and thus continually attacked with a straight (standard) Taekwon-Do Obverse Punch and nothing else, so of course, I had little chance to demonstrate many of the self defence skills I had against various other, more realistic, attacks.

1 Step Sparring is a wholly more standard way of training. In both 1 Step Sparring and Hosinsul practice you bow to your partner as a way of showing your respect to each other, as well as acknowledging you are going to practice correctly and that's where the similarities end.

In 1 Step Sparring, the attacker will start in either a Parallel Ready Stance or, if using an older system of Taekwon-Do, a Walking Stance. In some cases the defender will 'kihap' to show he is ready and then the attacker will 'kihap' as they attack.

In 1 Step Sparring the attack is often performed on the right side first, then repeated on the left side, with exactly the same attack. Many schools only use Middle Obverse Punch as an attack, where as others, like mine, allow any technique as an attack, such as Knifehands, Back-fists and Kicks.

In the practice of Hosinsul there is no formal stance the attacker must assume, nor is there a formal stance required for the defender. Some naturally form a Parallel Ready Stance, due to their 'Step Sparring' experiences, but this is not necessary and more so is bad practice for self defence.

In Hosinsul there is no need for the defender to let the attacker know that they are ready, just like a real life situation, the defender should be ready from the moment the Hosinsul practice session starts. The attacker can attack whenever they wish to, with no prior warning or waiting for the

Typical 1 Step Sparring

Typical 1 Step Sparring continued

defender to be ready. This may be with a prescribed and agreed upon technique or any technique the attacker wishes to use, depending on the way you are practicing Hosinsul at that time.

In 1 Step Sparring the attacker attacks with purely Taekwon-do techniques, from Obverse Punches to, if allowed, High Reverse Turning Kicks or any other traditional technique. Whereas in Hosinsul, attacks would be more 'street' related techniques, the kind of attack a non-Taekwon-Do student would likely use, such as throat grabs, headlocks, swinging hook punches or other more unorthodox attacks.

In 1 Step Sparring, if you strictly follow General Choi's system to the letter, it is one attack (held out by the attacker), followed by either a block or a dodge and a single counter attack, to a vital point, by the defender, though many schools allow more than a single counter-attack. 1 Step Sparring is also used to display the defenders skill in utilising kicking combinations i.e. a side step from a Punch, followed by a Turning Kick and then a Reverse Turning Kick.

In Hosinsul, both the attacking and defensive techniques will be markedly different from those you will see in 1 Step Sparring, as the student is practicing realistic street type attacks and the defences will mostly be close-quarters defences, whereas 1 Step Sparring defences are mostly confined to middle and long range counter-attacks.

In Hosinsul you are not restricted to a single counter attack, your defence will often consist of the initial response to the attack (defend or release), followed by a number of counter-strikes to nullify or finish your opponent.

In 1 Step Sparring both the attacks and defences, with the exception of a blocking technique are in the main, non-contact. The defender is supposed to show excellent control with his counter-attacks, so as not to hurt his training partner.

In Hosinsul, some contact is not only normal but should be expected, its actually an essential requirement to prepare the student for a real life encounter, after all, all the techniques in the world are no good if you drop like a stone or freeze when someone hits you for real!

Of course, contact levels can vary and techniques must be executed with safety in mind, for example, I expect my students to make some contact if they execute a Front Snap Kick as part of their defence, but they are not allowed to make contact with a headbutt, so in this case, the defending student should understand the effects a headbutt would have on them and adjust what they are doing accordingly. In this way, virtually every technique you can think of can be used as part of your Hosinsul practice.

Finally, when performed by two athletic students, 1 Step Sparring can look very artistic, almost like a Taekwon-Do ballet, where as Hosinsul isn't meant to look pretty, it is meant to be effective, often brutally so!

Whilst many may see 1 Step Sparring as more advanced than the practice of Hosinsul, General Choi actually saw it the other way around, stating that *'These techniques are not only the most interesting in Taekwon-Do, but also the most advanced'*.[8] His theory was that as the student trains from the very beginning towards 2nd Kup and beyond, many elements of training have been working towards becoming proficient in Hosinsul. From the simple clenching of a correctly formed fist, to executing kicks well, fitness and conditioning work and so on. Even 1 Step Sparring was considered a stepping stone towards successful Hosinsul, which is why, in his manuals, he placed the practice and testing of 1 Step Sparring starting at 6th Kup level, so it preceded more formal Hosinsul training, which was tested at 2nd Kup level, with the practice of Free-Sparring in between, at 4th Kup level. As Hosinsul became a more specialised training practice, students were introduced to two more methods of defence, to add to their 'attacking' motions (meaning defences using strikes). These were 'releasing' motion (releasing from grips and grabs) and 'breaking' motion (joint manipulation) and all these elements were allowed within formal Hosinsul training.

Also, do not confuse the real practice of Hosinsul with other areas of Taekwon-Do, such as the 'tournament' divisions often termed 'Pre-Arranged Self Defence' or 'Pre-Arranged Free Sparring' (which are both similar divisions by different names), 'Model Sparring' or anything else, such as a 'demonstration' of Hosinsul. If its pre-planned, then it is a performance, not true Hosinsul.

The Difference Between Boon Hae and Hosinsul

Whilst both Boon Hae (applications to patterns) and Hosinsul (self defence

---

[8] Encyclopedia of Taekwon-Do by General Choi Hong Hi; Chapter 5 - Self-Defence Techniques (Hosin Sul)

techniques) are inter-related, its the way they are taught that is different.

Boon Hae is basically showing how movements from a pattern (tul) can be used as a self defence technique and in what way, whereas Hosinsul would do this in reverse, showing how to defend against a certain type of attack, using a technique found within the patterns, non-pattern techniques or a mixture of both.

Students may (and should) study Boon Hae and use that in their Hosinsul practice, as without knowing a realistic application to a pattern technique, it would be impossible to use it reversed, in Hosinsul! Furthermore, Boon Hae is usually a lot more in-depth in the applications of it's techniques, as you follow the actual pattern movements, which apart from being the initial defences, often continue (as in the patterns themselves) into follow up techniques or in some cases, redundancy techniques, where as in Hosinsul, you can use a move or two from a pattern, then flow into anything else that is applicable.

Therefore, both areas of study are advised and useful.

When To Train Hosinsul

Opinions vary on this, some feel it should be taught right from the very beginning of a student's training, whereas others feel it should be taught later on, once a student has gained a good foundation in the art and has a good grasp of fundamental techniques; after all it no use teaching someone to counter-punch, when they don't even know how to form a fist correctly!

As I stated earlier, General Choi believed the practice of formal Hosinsul shouldn't be graded until 2nd Kup, however I personally feel that its practice should start around 4th Kup, as by then, students have a good foundation and are acquiring good techniques which they can apply in Hosinsul, as well as learning new and useful techniques, not often used in other area's of training, such as knee's and elbows, expanding their repertoire considerably.

How To Train Hosinsul

Watching some videos on Youtube over the years, I have seen Hosinsul taught in a variety of ways; many of which were not conducive to a student really learning how to defend themselves from a real attacker, as the students went through various self defence techniques with no resistance from the attacker whatsoever and whilst this may be okay for a basic introduction, more senior students should be both attacking and defending with more force, more commitment, more resistance and more realism.

Chapter 1:
The Practice of Hosinsul

I have seen Taekwon-do schools teach Hosinsul with set attacks and defences, sometimes numbering up to 50 or more, namely the attacker grabs and the defender must do this exact counter-attack, with more and more added as they move up the grades. Personally, I find this approach unnecessary, as students should, over time, find out what the best and most natural defences are for themselves, from ideas taught to them by their instructors and fellow students and while the approach I mention here seems similar, it is not, as its more a mental memory test, than actually applying and practicing techniques that would work in a real life situation.

There is no 'one size fits all' when it comes to Hosinsul, different students have different attributes, different strengths and different weaknesses. Some may be much taller than others, or much stronger, some more flexible or agile, some quite heavy, others very light. Some may be more comfortable or better at using certain techniques than others. Over time, students will figure out what works best for them, and will often end up using the same or similar techniques over and over, which is a good thing, as it prevents a log-jam effect, which you really don't want when you have to react in a self-defence situation.

With that said, as students often teach other students and/or become instructors, it is useful to know other ways of practice, so the 12 stone, bulky male instructor can advise and teach the slighter student techniques and defences that may be more applicable to them.

In my opinion, the best way to teach Hosinsul to start with, is to present a certain type of attack and a few options of defence against it and allow the student to try them out and practice with them. This may include having a list of prescribed attacks, but not of actual, set in stone, defences. After all, as I said, a large muscled male student will most likely chose different defences than a small female student, a confident kicker will use their legs more than a student who is not so confident and so on, so it is pointless forcing them to do things in overly defined ways, that are in opposition to their natural body types and contrary to their instincts and skills.

It is important to stress that Hosinsul should be realistic in nature, in both attack and defence, which is why having a list to start with can help, as students who don't quite understand the purpose will often do nonsensical attacks, such as Flying Reverse Turning Kicks that you are unlikely to see in a street attack scenario. The same is true of the defences, with students performing unrealistic counter-attacks, that in reality would get them hurt should they try it for real, against someone who is actually committed to hurting them.

In this book, you will not find attacking techniques that you are unlikely to encounter in a real attack, you will of course see many Taekwon-Do techniques as defences, but not techniques that could never realistically be used (by the majority) in self defence. In fact, almost all the attacking techniques in this book are based on HAOV (Habitual Acts of Violence), a study listing the most common street attacks by Sensei Patrick McCarthy.

Once a student has gained a good grounding in basic Hosinsul, then training should move forwards. Any 'known' attack should be executed with more speed, aggression and realism, adding in some resistance to counter-attacks (meaning the attacker should be forced to comply and not just comply for the sake of it). Finally, there should be no 'pre-determined' attacks at all, just attacks from the front, rear and maybe the side.

Elements Of Successful Hosinsul

Apart from the actual techniques themselves, there are certain elements that you should consider and train to give you the best chance of success as possible. These are:

- *Reaction* - Fast reactions are a vital element in self defence, as the quicker you respond to an attack, the more the likelihood of a successful outcome. In the early stages students may pause and think about what techniques they will do to defend themselves, however, with time and practice this gap will decrease as students come to understand how techniques work and practice them through repetition. Other areas of Taekwon-Do will also help you train your reflexes and reaction skills, such as 1 Step Sparring and any kind of competition based Free Sparring.

- *Speed* - Speed is of course the cousin of reaction. The quicker you are able to apply your defence, the better chance you have of pulling it off. Obviously the more you practice a technique, the faster it will become, until eventually you execute it by instinct alone.

- *Surprise* - Whilst it may be impossible to replicate in the dojang, as everybody knows what they are doing, surprise is in fact your secret ally on the street. In the main, 'victims' are usually people that an aggressor considers an easy target, and thus can defeat easily. When an aggressor feels in control, they often drop their (metaphorical) guard and become over-confident, which becomes a weakness to exploit, so you keep this element until you need it. This means keeping relaxed. Confidence gained through training Hosinsul will allow you to remain relaxed and comfortable within your training, thus not giving away your secret too early. Maintaining this element also means not showing you know martial arts, so do not form a fighting stance and do not raise your hands into a clenched fist guard or any form of recognisable formal defence preparation - use a 'Fence' instead.

- *Aggression* - Aggression is an important element for successful self defence. When you use your Hosinsul for real, you react to the situation, surprising your attacker whilst applying your defence with speed and aggression. You have to learn to be aggressive in the dojang.

- *Intent* - When you are defending yourself, you must have the intent to take it as far as needed, you must 'intend' all your techniques to really do damage, you cannot be half hearted in what you are doing, because if you are, you will 'pull' your defensive techniques and then you will be defeated.

- *Toughness* - A bit of toughness goes a long way. Whilst some people are naturally tough, usually because of life itself and others 'get tough' through fighting, the average student is not, so toughening yourself up should be a priority in all of your training. The next time you are sparring and someone hits you a lot harder than expected, try to shrug it off rather than complain. If you get knocked on your butt, don't spend 5 minutes having a break, get yourself back up on your feet and back in the fight. If you do 50 press-ups in class, push yourself past it and do 55. If you are out of breath when sparring, ignore it and carry on - generally push yourself that extra bit more than your usual comfort zone. Of course, all this with safety in mind! Toughness can also be gained through the practice of Hosinsul itself, by simply adding a little bit more contact and aggression.

Safety In Practice

Of course, it's all well and good saying increase the contact, up your levels of aggression and the levels of associated pressure, but in the dojang, you are practicing Hosinsul with a training partner, who is a fellow student, so some safety precautions need to be applied.

Some instructors like to use 'full body protection' suits, such as the bullet man or redman suits, but I personally find this counter-productive on a number of levels, as they cover the attacking student too well and thus make strikes to vital points such as the eyes ineffective and they also nullify the defenders harder shots, that in reality would have done some damage to the aggressor.

Others prefer the use of some padding, such as shin and forearm guards, and full face head guards, again, for the same reasons as above, they limit what the defender can do and what they can counter-attack with. For example, a strike to the shin is rendered ineffective by the simple wearing of a shin pad.

Above all, real attackers are unlikely to be wearing any form of body protection above and beyond standard, everyday clothing and consequently nor will you, the defender!

In my opinion, it is better to understand the *cause and effect* of certain defences that you simply cannot do with 100% realness within the dojang. For example, a light press with my thumbs on my opponents eyes constitutes an eye gouge and my opponent should recognise this and react appropriately, for example, releasing a grip. For an actual eye strike I aim at the forehead, for kicks to the side of the knee, I only lightly tap it and I make similar adjustments for other vital points whilst retaining the reality of performance.

With most strikes you can make some contact, just not full contact. Even some light to medium contact often gains the natural response that a full contact strike would. For example, a knee to the stomach with some contact will still make them bend forwards and try to cover with their arms in case a second knee strike is coming, allowing an attack to the head or other targets.

Chokes and locking techniques can be practiced relatively safely, by use of the 'double tap' system, provided students are well versed in them to begin with.

Throws and take downs are relatively safe to execute, so long as the student knows how to breakfall safely and of course execute the throws properly.

Students practicing throwing techniques

The trick is to find a level of contact that's viable for those practicing Hosinsul, making it a little rough, but not dangerous and ensure everyone knows the *'cause and effect'* of the techniques that can't make real contact, such as a Circular Elbow to the jaw, which would at the very least shock and stun an attacker or, if used at full force break their jaw or likely knock them out altogether, ending the attack.

Don't Run Before You Can Walk

In order to have a full arsenal of techniques for your Hosinsul practice, as well as (and more importantly), to be able to execute them safely, it is important to practice certain techniques in isolation first, to ensure proficiency in basic techniques which are the bedrock of good Hosinsul.

Students practising knee techniques on the pads

By the time most Taekwon-Do students will be practicing Hosinsul they will be well versed in punching (and other hand strikes) and kicking, but should also practice:

The 'double tap'

- Break falls
- Throwing techniques
- Sweeping techniques
- Joint locking techniques
- Choking techniques
- Knee techniques
- Elbow techniques
- 'Other' techniques not often practised (such as eye gouges)
- Vital points and their effects
- The 'double tap'[9]

Instructors may or may not include some or all of the above aspects as part of class training, but if not, they should seek to include them for partner practice and all should be taught and practiced under a competent instructor.

Those practising Hosinsul should also know the effects of certain strikes, how much contact is allowed (or safe to use with certain techniques), what techniques shouldn't be used directly and what a normal reaction to them would likely be.

---

[9] The 'double tap' is a safety measure used when practicing joint locks and chokes, whereby the student 'double taps' his training partner, who then immediately releases the technique.

Students practising various elbow techniques on the pads

To make Hosinsul fully complete, some 'ground work' should be taught and trained as well!

The Conundrum of Hosinsul

As an instructor, knowing lots of Hosinsul is great, as it enables you to offer alternatives to students, to try out and practice themselves, to find the right ones for them. However, for you, as a student, you don't want to create a log-jam effect when you have to defend yourself, as you want to instinctively react to the attack and not slow yourself down by having to think through which counter-attack to use.

Consequently, you will find, as training in Hosinsul continues, most students will find 'their way'; their preferred method of successfully dealing with an attack, whatever it may be. This method will often be repeated for different types of attacks as well, as its their instinct kicking in. This is good for a student's self defence, as that's ideally what we want to achieve - a successful defence, applied by a student who is fully competent in its use and fully confident when using it and thus isn't having to think about it at all.

You will also find that whilst students may react with different defences to various attacks, i.e. they would not use the same initial defence to a rear bear hug attack, as they would for a hay-maker type hooking punch, their follow up (finishing) techniques will often be the same, over and over - again this is natural and a good trait to have.

Angles of Attack and Defence

Many attacks (in real life) follow a basic scenario; first of all there is shouting or an argument, often some shoving or pushing, then a grab followed by a strike or just the strike itself.

As most attacks start with some form of verbal abuse, we, as the defender, will turn to face the aggressor, so we would be in front of them and thus the majority of our Hosinsul practice starts from this position.

However, though frontal attacks may be the most common, we of course need to learn to defend against attacks from the rear and side.

In defence, we may defend ourselves in a central position, straight in front of our opponent, using surprise, speed, aggression and full intent to take the advantage, but we can add to that advantage by moving to the outside of our opponent, as this makes using one of the aggressors hands as another strike or grab, so much harder.

Moving to the outside of the attacker

Consequently, if we can get behind the attacker, by either moving or turning them, then we have a major advantage of not only being able to apply a choke or strike vital points in the back, but also making it even more difficult for them to use their 'standard' attacking tools i.e. their fists. Though we must always remain aware of rear elbow strikes and flailing arms. There is an old saying: *'Take the back, win the fight'*, so when viable, in a real situation, its always a good idea to get a choke on and keep it on, no matter what happens!

Getting behind an opponent offers a major advantage

Knees, Elbows And Other Nasty Things

Most students rarely think of using knee strikes or elbows in the dojang unless they actively train them at some point, which is a shame, as they are some of our strongest weapons and relatively easy to use, compared to things like turning kicks and other conventional blows.

The comparative ease of using knees and elbows at close quarters means that they are ideal to use in many situations and are often the prerequisite follow up techniques of choice, following a successful release from a grab or hold, but they can also be used instead of a release, when a student doesn't know what to do, to simply batter an opponent until they release their grip.

In Ch'ang Hon Taekwon-Do there are at least 8 different types of single elbow techniques; upper, front, side, rear, downwards, turning, angular (known as high elbow), spinning, plus some of their 'twin' variations. Some are easily identifiable within the patterns, whilst for others you have to look a little harder!

Most instructors feel that students do not come across knee techniques until they are learning Toi-Gye tul, but for the open minded instructor, it actually appears within patterns, as early as 7th kup, when the student starts to practice Do-San tul and even earlier during the practice of fundamental techniques, even if not practicing knee kicks directly, as a basic knee kick is just a front snap kick that doesn't extend the lower half of the leg! On top of that, we can also use turning knee kicks and side knee kicks, as counter techniques.

Other techniques may or may not appear within the patterns depending on your perspective, but shouldn't be discounted either. In some circles they may be considered 'dirty' techniques, but in the realm of self defence they might just be the one technique that turns defeat into victory. These are biting, gouging, headbutts, groin grabs, various joint manipulations, choking, strangulations, ripping and even spitting!

When It All Goes Wrong!

Once a student has a number of Hosinsul techniques under their belt, they should start training them without knowing what the opponent may attack them with, so subsequently they won't know what techniques they will use as their defence so things begin to become instinctual.

Of course, mistakes will happen and the student will sometimes pick the wrong techniques or those that they do try, won't work, so what they often do is stop, reset and start again - but this is a mistake, as there is a valuable lesson to learn and practice here!

When (and inevitably they will) things go wrong, the student should learn to adapt to the situation and try something else. After all, it is better to fail in the dojang than it is for real, but even for real, things can easily go wrong, so learning to quickly adapt, recover and carry on is a vital component to Hosinsul and another aspect that will take the dojang training another step closer to reality.

So, just remember; *'When it all goes wrong... ... take the hit and carry on'*

Free Sparring

Whilst not part of Hosinsul practice, free sparring (or a better term would be fighting) is what happens in real life when self-defence doesn't work as we hoped, therefore we have to fight.

In many classes 'free sparring' is only viewed as the type you would practice for tournaments and whilst some of the attributes will be helpful in a real fight and indeed, some of the better tournament fighters would probably do just fine, for the average student it is far removed from the realism of a real fight, contact is much lower, many techniques are not allowed, grabbing is not allowed at all and the onus is on scoring points, as opposed to finishing the opponent as quickly as possible.

In class, allowing more contact sometimes can be useful, as it allows students to see how they react under such conditions, shows them they can in fact 'take a hit' properly, however it still leaves a lot of elements unaddressed, which is why, in my classes we do both 'competition' sparring (to prepare for tournaments) and 'traditional' sparring; a form of sparring so named, as it allows much more use of traditional techniques, well beyond the scope of what tournament rules allow.

Traditional Sparring

Traditional Sparring is an 'all in' type of sparring. When training it, students are allowed to punch, kick, grab, throw, sweep, execute locks and chokes and even fight on the ground for a certain amount of time. Students wear minimal padding (such as a mouth guard only), nothing is off limits providing it is executed in a safe manner.

Apart from being more realistically like a 'fight', one of the first things I emphasise is that its 'training', there are no winners or losers; providing you learn something or work on something, each time you do it, everybody wins. And with that mindset, it allows students to utilise certain techniques in a safe manner, that they usually wouldn't be able or allowed to use.

For example; Whilst training traditional sparring, a student rushes in and starts to execute a double leg takedown. In a real situation, I may execute a downward elbow strike to the attackers spine, but of course, I cannot (and wouldn't) do that in training, as its very dangerous, so instead, as he is lifting me off the floor, I simulate the same strike, but using the back of my upper arm (the tricep area, so its flat and not pointed), striking down to his shoulder blade area instead of his spine. I still get taken down with that defence, but I know, whilst its all going on I was able to smash it down 3 or 4 times and so I know, if that was for real, that would have been the point of my elbow, smashing into my opponents back and spine, damaging him considerably. On the surface it may look like I lost, but I won (for myself) as it showed that, if for real, I could use that technique to damage my opponent.

Example 2; I have ended up grappling with a stronger opponent and he is trying to get a choke or strangle on me, so I thrust my arms forward and press my thumbs either very lightly on his eyes or heavier to his eyebrows! We both understand that this is what we use to simulate an eye-gouge (meaning pressing my thumbs as hard and deep into the attackers eyes as possible). It would be a game changer in a real fight, as the opponent would be blinded (even if temporarily), his hands would have stopped trying to choke me as they grabbed my attacking arms to counter my gouging, which would have allowed me to throw follow up techniques. So we stop, reset and start a new round - its really that simple when you understand it.

Of course, the previous examples are just some 'exceptions' for safety purposes, in the main, most techniques can be done at full speed, with a reasonable amount of power. This allows a good kicker to be nullified by grappling, a puncher to be taken down with a throw, a good grappler having to try his grips whilst being punched and other scenario's, taking both partners out of their comfort zones. It even allows a students to see if the Taekwon-Do techniques he regularly uses in tournaments, would work in a more realistic 'fight' type situation.

These days, we have replaced standard sparring gloves, with grappling gloves, so we can both strike and grab effectively.

Cross Referencing Defences

Whist this book gives multiple options of techniques to use against various attacks, with a little cross-referencing within its pages, you will actually find even more than is actually printed here, as many of the defences can be used against a multitude of attacks.

For example, the defences against a two handed front choke can be used exactly the same against two handed shoulder grabs or double lapel grabs. Defences against straight punches can be used against single push attacks, single lapel grabs or an attempted single handed choke and many more examples will become apparent as training progresses.

In the end, the same or similar defence, useful for a variety of situations, means in real life, everything requires less thought, leaving you more time to simply react and thus more likely that your techniques will work effectively.

"If you're going through hell, keep going!"

- Winston Churchill

Chapter 2
Before We Begin

The 'Fence'

The 'Fence' is a technique I first came across in the early 1990's via Self Protection expert Geoff Thompson's book 'Real Self Defence' (now re-released as 'Dead or Alive: The Choice Is Yours), which was, in my opinion (and as it says on the books cover) the *definitive* handbook on Self Protection - back in the 90's and possibly still to this day.

The Fence is a technique designed to maintain a safer distance between you and an aggressor, as it allows the defender reaction time from attempted grabs, strikes and sucker punches, without, in itself, looking aggressive and thus heightening any given situation, allowing it to perhaps be diffused before anything physical happens. It can also be used to judge the distance for a strike if a situation looks like it is about to get physical, allowing the defender a 'pre-emptive strike'.

The Staggered Fence

As the use of the Fence is obviously related to Hosinsul, and thus is a must have tool in a students tool box of techniques, not only are there different type of Fence that students can utilize, it is also a good idea, when practicing Hosinsul, that students do away with the old postures of standing in parallel ready stance, with the hands in front of their bellies and instead adopt a Fence type posture, as its more realistic for a real world encounter and it allows for a much better reaction time when attacked, even if just in practice. More so, using the Fence often, will mean the student will utilise it immediately should they have to deal with a real aggressor.

The Exclamation Fence

As part of self protection practice often requires some acting ability, different Fences suit different students, depending on their confidence levels and their aforementioned acting ability.

My personal favourite is the 'Exclamation Fence' as it looks like you are questioning why someone is being so aggressive, others may prefer the 'Staggered' Fence, which looks like you are simply saying 'woah... hold on mate', whilst someone who is less confident or in a very fearful situation, may opt to use a 'Pleading' Fence as, out of all the various Fence

The Pleading Fence

postures, this one is most likely to make an attacker drop his psychological guard the most, allowing a pre-emptive strike to be that bit more effective.

Apart from the physical Fences shown here, ones which can be practiced with your standard Hosinsul training, there are also 'Verbal' Fences, 'Psychological' Fences, 'Invisible' Fences and even a 'Negative' Fence, but these are beyond the scope of this book , but are detailed very well in the aforementioned book by Geoff Thompson.

As I said in my very first book, for those who deem this type of technique 'non-traditional' simply look at a standard Knifehand Guarding Block and you will see they are pretty similar.

You will notice that throughout this book I often employ a Fence coupled with a small 45 degree stance, both are designed to look 'non-aggressive' and whilst the Fence allows me to maintain some form of control, the small 45 degree stance allows me to strike (perhaps pre-emptively) utilising the power of my hips or at the very least, gives me a better base to react from, so I am not immediately thrown off balance by an aggressor.

Using A Fence And Pre-Emptive Striking

For most (but not all) Fences, your front hand is used to maintain a gap between you and the aggressor, without looking like an aggressive action itself. As a situation starts to become aggressive and an assailant moves towards you, the student would put up a Fence as a barrier between themselves and the aggressor.

As (or if) the assailant becomes even more aggressive and continues moving forwards (usually meaning an attack is imminent) the student can step backwards (whilst still holding their Fence), maintaining the distance and at some point, if needed, strike pre-emptively.

Using the 'fence' with a pre-emptive strike

As well as the standard right cross or hook punch, a few other examples of pre-emptive strikes that work well, depending on range, are palm strikes, palm slaps, forearm smashes, knee kicks, low kicks, front kicks, elbow strikes, arc-hand strikes and headbutts.

*Pre-emptive
Palm Strike*

Pre-emptive Turning Elbow Strike

*A Pre-emptive Palm Strike or Slap,
commonly referred to as a 'Power Slap'*

Pre-emptive Knee Kick   *Pre-emptive Front Headbutt*

Pre-emptive Forearm Smash

Pre-emptive Low Turning Kick, using the Shin

Pre-emptive Arc-Hand Strike

Of course, it goes without saying that students should learn about, as well as practice variations of the Fence and pre-emptive striking, as well as being educated on why they are allowed in self-defence situations where reasonable force becomes the only available option, as well as where they stand within the laws of their country.

Keeping An Aggressive Opponent At Bay

While the Fence is a great way of maintaining distance with an opponent if they are being aggressive but have yet to attack you, what do you do if an aggressor is already coming at you, from a distance, with the intention of striking or grabbing you?

You could simply engage them of course, or you could try to keep them at bay, whilst softening them up and possibly one of the best ways to keep a moving opponent at bay is by using a low side pressing or piercing kick.

As the opponent comes at you aggressively, quickly execute a hard side kick to their upper thigh off your front leg. As it's a low kick, its hard to grab and it keeps their hands out of range for grabs or hand strikes.

Ensure each time you kick it is fast, hard and retracted quickly (don't bounce on one leg like tournament fighters do).

Keep moving and only execute the kick when needed and be warned that this will only work for a short while, so be prepared to run or fight when the opportunity arises.

Precursor Techniques For Strikes

A 'precursor technique' is a technique they precedes the main technique, in order to make it work more effectively. Whilst throwing a right cross (for example) from a fence may catch an opponent off guard and thus work for us effectively, what if the opponent is already 'on guard'? If so, we can use a precursor technique to illicit a certain response and action from our opponent, clearing the way for our real strike.

Think of the movies, where one opponent will throw something in the air to the other person and they automatically throw their hands up to catch it, leaving them open for a front kick to the stomach. However, real precursor techniques can do much more than that!

You will read more about precursor technique preceding the 'releasing from grabs and chokes' chapters, as the techniques used there are different to those that precede strikes, but here are some to aid your striking techniques against an aggressor, should you need them and they are easily practiced with focus pads or similar.

Face Cover

Either as an aggressive opponent moves forwards or as part of a pre-emptive strike, the student uses the front hand to cover the opponents face, blinding him temporarily so that the 'take out' technique; the punch to the aggressors throat, is clear to travel to its intended target.

Finger Flick

A simple flick of the students fingers into the aggressors eyes is a simple, yet very effective way of distracting the opponent as it works on natural human reflexes. Think of what happens when you get a tiny bit of dust in your eye? Everything stops immediately to clear it out, you squint your eye and bring your hands to it in order to clear the dust out and this is the response the finger flick achieves.

Prior to your own pre-emptive attack, simply flick your fingers towards your opponents eyes. Even if you don't actually make contact, the opponent will still likely bring their hands up to defend against it and it will obscure their vision temporarily, allowing for your real strike to hit its target - in this case a low front snap kick.

Finger Jab

As your front hand is pretty close to the attacker, using a straight finger jab to the eyes is a great way to temporarily disable your opponent allowing you to follow up with a more powerful technique. With luck, it may be enough to end a confrontation altogether.

Fakes

Faking A Front Punch To Allow The Kick To Hit The Target

Faking A Kick To Allow The Punch To Hit The Target

Just like in normal sparring, fake techniques are great for raising or lowering an opponents defence. Working on the high/low principle (throwing a higher technique will naturally raise their guard and throwing a low technique will lower their guard), the student can fake a punch, but hit hard with a front or rising kick to the attackers groin.

Alternatively, the student can fake a kick, in order to enable the punch a better chance of making solid contact with the opponents jaw.

"Of old, the expert in battle would first make himself invincible and then wait for his enemy to expose his vulnerability."

~ Sun Tzu

Chapter 3
Defences Against Hand Strikes

Defences Against Straight Punches

A straight punch (often termed a non-uniformed punch) is any hand technique that travels in a straight forwards direction, such as a 'straight right' punch or a 'right cross' punch. It isn't performed as a standard Taekwon-Do punch (as in from the hip) and can be executed with or without a step forward.

Though easy to counter if you know they are coming, in real life, due to the fact they travel in a straight line, the time you have to react is a lot less, so having a 'fence' is very important to enable some distance between you and the aggressor and thus give you a bit more reaction time.

Straight Punch - Defence 1

For this defence, we use a low turning kick, striking with the shin.

1. Keep your distance from the attacker by use of a fence.

2. As the straight punch comes forwards, drop your body down, whilst twisting to the side, to take you out of the direct line of attack.

3a & 3b. As you do so (step 2) immediately counter-attack by executing a low turning kick to the attackers legs, preferably the thigh or knee joint, with your shin.

5, 6 & 7. If possible, grab hold of the attackers arm and continue your counter-attacks with strikes of your own such as punches (6) or elbows (7).

Straight Punch - Defence 2

For this defence, we react by side stepping whilst simultaneously using a palm hooking block, as first found in Yul-Gok tul.

1a, 1b & 1c. As the attacker throws their punch (with or without a step forwards), immediately take yourself our of the direct line of attack, by side stepping to the outside of the punch, whilst at the same time executing a palm hooking block to grab onto the attackers arm.

2a & 2b. Immediately execute a turning kick to the attackers abdomen.

3a & 3b. Re-chamber your leg and execute a side pressing kick to the side of the attackers knee.

4a & 4b. Complete your counter-attack by executing a reverse knifehand strike (or forearm strike) to the rear of the attackers head. ***Note:*** *Do not strike your training partner with this technique as there are vital points at the base of the skull that can cause death if hit hard.*

Straight Punch - Defence 3

This is a less lethal defence and it is executed utilising the L-Stance with obverse punch that first appears in Hwa-Rang tul to create a triangle choke.

1a & 1b. As the attacker throws their punch, slip into an L-Stance (taking you out of the direct line of attack), whilst parrying the blow with your front hand.

2. Immediately execute the obverse punch to the attackers floating ribs. (optional)

3. Immediately after the punch bring your arm up and to the side of the attackers throat, along their carotid artery. Or, you can omit the punch altogether and go straight for the strangle technique, depending on distance and reaction.

4. Grab hold of your fist, whilst placing your head and shoulder onto the opposite side of the attackers body and head (parallel to your other arm) and squeeze tightly.

Front view of 4

5. As you apply the triangle choke, drop down onto one knee whilst pulling your attacker down with you.

Straight Punch - Defence 4

This defence is a combination block and counter technique, that black belts will recognise as being directly from the 1st Dan tul, Po-Eun.

1a, 1b & 1c. As the punch is thrown, slip into an L-Stance (taking you out of the direct line of attack) and using the horizontal punch from Po-Eun tul, block the actual punch with your rear arm, whilst simultaneously attacking the attackers throat with your lead arm, striking at their throat..

2a & 2b. At this point, you can counter attack with strikes, but you can also follow the flow of the pattern (Po-Eun tul) by grabbing the attackers arm and pulling it downwards as you step forwards, twisting it as you do so (so the palm is outwards) and striking it with your opposite arm, to break the elbow joint.

Defences Against Hooking Punches

A hooking or hook punch is any hand technique that travels in a circular motion, obviously it would have a closed fist if a punch, but the same can be applied to any circular strike performed with the arm, such as an open handed slap.

There are two types of hook punches, the 'haymaker' variety that is wound up and travels in a wide arc, giving plenty of reaction time and the closer range hook punch, that is harder to deal with due to the limited reaction time.

Haymaker Hooking Punch - Defence 1
This defence uses the wedging block found in Do-San tul and has an advantage for the weaker student, as it can be either a single handed or double handed defence.

1a, 1b & 1c. As the attacker throws their haymaker hooking punch, turn into it and execute the outer forearm wedging block from Do-San tul. If you mistimed your defence, you still have both hands up to block the punch. If you are confident, you can block the punch with one arm, whilst simultaneously striking the carotid artery of your opponent with your other arm. Alternatively, you can simply block with both arms, then strike the opponents carotid artery immediately after, with your inside arm.

2a & 2b. Immediately follow up (just like in the pattern) with a front rising kick (2a) to the attackers groin. Alternatively, depending on your distance, you can use a knee instead (2b), though I actually prefer to

use the front snap kick, straight to the attackers femoral artery on their inside thigh, as the angle we are at, allows this follow through very easily.

Haymaker Hooking Punch - Defence 2

For this defence, we start by using a combination first found in Won-Hyo tul and turn it into a figure 4 arm lock.

1a, 1b & 1c. As the attacker throws the punch, turn into it and block it with your rear arm (at the forearm), whilst simultaneously striking at the attackers neck or face with your front arm.

2a & 2b. After striking the opponent with your lead arm, immediately retract it and strike the inside of the opponents elbow joint, whilst pressing forwards with your other arm in order to bend the opponents elbow.

3a, 3b, 3c & 3d. From this position, loop your right hand through and around onto your left arm to form the figure 4 lock. (See close up shots, 3b,

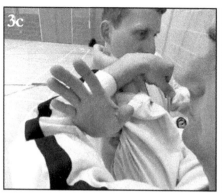

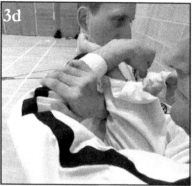

3c & 3d)

4a & 4b. With the figure 4 lock on, drop your weight directly downwards, taking the opponent to the ground.

Haymaker Hooking Punch - Defence 3

For this defence, we use a knifehand guarding block found in Dan-Gun tul.

1. As the attacker winds up their punch, keep your hands up and prepare to defend.

2. As the haymaker punch travels round towards you, turn your body into the punch.

3a, 3b & 3c. Use the chambering position of a knifehand guarding block to stop the punch. Aiming to hit both the radial nerve and the

bicep at the same time (3b). Ensuring you use the follow through of the block to add impact and damage to the opponents arm (3c).

4a & 4b. Follow up immediately with the actual 'blocking' part of the technique, using the front hand to strike at the opponents carotid artery and the other to trap their arm (if possible), by wrapping it around and under.

5a & 5b. Following directly on from the knifehand strike, loop your front hand around the back of the opponents head and pull it down as you execute a knee kick to their stomach.

6a & 6b. Following up with an elbow strike to the back of the attackers head.

Haymaker Hooking Punch - Defence 4

For this defence, we use a simple knifehand block but use our own rotation to turn the block into a shoulder throw.

1a & 1b. As the attackers punch comes around towards you, move inside it, blocking it with a knifehand block.

2. Immediately pivot anti-clockwise and hook your other arm under the attackers armpit/arm, whilst grabbing hold of the attackers front arm.

3. Maintain your grip on the attackers arm, pushing your opposite arm upwards to secure the hold whilst bending your knees (and breaking the opponents balance, if needed, by 'bucking' your hips into them).

4a & 4b. With the opponent 'hooked' start the throw by bending forwards whilst straightening your legs.

5a & 5b. Once you have thrown them in front, complete your defence by immediately dropping your weight down onto them via your knee.

6. Alternatively (or additionally), if you have hold of the attackers arm following the

throw, you can twist into a low block position and break their elbow by crashing it (whilst locked straight) into your front knee.

Defences Against Close Range Punches

Close range punches are notoriously difficult to combat due to the limited reaction time the defender has. For the most part, the solution is simply to cover up and take the punch (on your arms), before counter attacking. On the plus side, most close range punches do not generate as much power as medium range ones, though can be just as devastating if they hit their mark, such as a close range upper cut to the jaw.

Any punch can be executed at close range and can roughly be split into two categories; 1) close range uppercuts and shovel punches (commonly known as upset punches in Taekwon-Do) and 2) close range hooks, straight and cross punches, as well as lead hand jabs. In this section we look at a few examples of defending against both types.

Close Range Uppercuts or Upset Punch - Defences

For close range defences against uppercuts and upset punches, the aim is to nullify the attack first, then immediately counter-attack and we do that by using an X-fist downward block that we first find in the 2nd degree tul, Eui-Am.

1a, 1b & 1c. As the attacker throws their close range upset punch (or uppercut), drop both arms down onto the incoming attack, using the X-fist downward block. Crossing them leaves very little room for the attack to slip through.

2a & 2b. Immediately execute your

counter attack, which can be anything you want, though in this example we have simply used the next move from the sequence in Eui-Am tul and used a knifehand rising block as a strike to the attackers jaw, as it flows very naturally.

3. Continuing our counter attack, we use a knee kick to the opponents groin or abdomen.

4a, 4b & 4c. Before finishing them off with an elbow strike to the back of the head.

Close Range Hooks or Straight Punch - Defences

Close range hooks and straight punches are very hard to defend against and thus require quite good reflexes in the student. On the following pages I offer techniques you can use if the punch actually hits, but if you are quick enough to react, you can use the high double forearm block that we first find at the end of Yul-Gok tul.

1a, 1b & 1c. As the punch comes in, bring both hands up high, whilst also raising your shoulder to cover your jaw and dipping your head. Tense your jaw as well and turn in towards the punch slightly, taking the power of the attackers punch on both your arms *(see right picture).*

Note: If it's a straight punch, you would slip to the side slightly.

2a & 2b. As you are already at very close range after blocking the punch, you can counter-attack with an elbow strike, this can be an upper elbow strike or (my preference) a side elbow strike, where we grab hold of the attackers arm and strike their head with our other elbow.

Defences Against Slaps

For the most part, a slap is more a shock technique than a take out technique. Though not always heavy on the contact, they can be fast and hard to stop and the further back the attacker chambers them, the stronger they usually are, but the easier they are to defend against. In a real situation, a slap can often be the first step to something much worse as a simple slap across the face triggers the 'fight or flight' response, which can make a victim 'freeze' as their bodies are flooded with adrenaline and thus unable to react to a situation as they should.

A slap can be with the palm or it can be a backhand slap, with the backhand version similar in motion to a backfist strike, so similar defences can be used. A slap with the palm travels in a similar fashion to a haymaker hooking punch and so similar defences can also be employed. Though you will read about 'power slaps' in this book, a standard slap is not the same as it travels in an arc type motion. Also, in anger, it is often pulled back before being released, telegraphing the technique.

Palm Slap - Defence 1
For this defence we use the outer forearm side block and reverse punch combination found in do-San tul.

1a & 1b. As soon as the attacker raises their hand, bring up your guard ready to intercept.

2. Depending on the situation, use your outer forearm side block to intercept, either as it is in the pattern (without the full chamber) or by simply raising it straight up.

3. Follow up with a straight right punch to the attackers jaw.

Backhand Slap - Defence 1

A backhand slap off the front hand is less powerful, but gives you a lot less reaction time, so for these defence we use a triangle block to absorb the slap, then counter with a right cross punch.

1a & 1b. As the backhand slap travels towards you, bring your hand up to just above your ear and turn away slightly, taking the backhand slap on your arm.

2. As soon as the slap hits, counter attack with your opposite arm, using a right cross punch.

Backhand Slap - Defence 2

Here we use a similar defence to the previous one, but as the backhand slap is executed from the attackers rear hand, we have a little more reaction time, so instead of just a parry, we utilise the palm hooking block found in Yul-Gok tul.

1a & 1b. As the attacker withdraws their hand ready to backhand slap you, bring up your closest arm and intercept the incoming attack with a palm hooking block, grabbing onto the attackers arm if possible.

2. Counter attack whilst still controlling the attackers arm, by using a reverse punch to their jaw.

Backhand Slap - Defence 3

Again we are going to use a palm hooking block found in Yul-Gok, to intercept and grab the incoming backhand slap, but this time we are going to follow up using a low outer forearm block to create an arm block.

1a & 1b. Intercept the incoming backhand slap with whatever arm is closest to it, forming a palm hooking block to grab hold of the attackers arm.

2a & 2b. As soon as you grab the arm, rotate it (so the point of the attackers elbow is facing upwards) whilst at the same time stepping in and executing a low outer forearm block to the attackers upper arm (above the elbow joint), pressing down with your forearm, forcing the attacker to the floor.

Defences Against Downward Strikes

A downward strike is any attacking technique that travels downwards towards the defender, usually towards their head from above. The actual attacking tool can be a side fist, a knifehand or even a weapon, though if a weapon is involved, the response, defence and counter techniques should be different to an empty hand attack.

Downward Strike - Defence 1

For this defence we use the outer forearm rising block from Dan-Gun tul and the upset fingertip thrust found in Toi-Gye tul.

1a & 1b. We intercept the attackers downward strike by moving in towards the attacker and executing the rising block to their tricep (upper arm).

2. After stopping the initial attack, we reach down with our other hand and execute a low fingertip thrust to their groin area.

3. Grab hold of either their scrotum or inner thigh and rip your hand backwards and upwards.

Downward Strike - Defence 2

For this defence we use an x-fist rising block, first found **in Joong-Gun tul,** followed by a foot sweep, similar to the one found in **Sam-Il tul, except we** execute it off the front leg.

1a & 1b. Intercept the attackers downward strike with an X-fist rising block.

2. Try and grip onto the attackers arm with one of your hands, whilst at the same time bringing your front foot behind the attackers front foot.

3a, 3b & 3c. Whilst maintaining hold of the attackers arm, keep the arm held high and execute a front foot sweep by bringing the attackers foot forwards and upwards at about a 45 degree angle using your inner footsword.

With the attackers arm held high, it will be more difficult for them to retain their balance, it can also be used to help the sweep by rotating their arm in the same direction as the attacker will fall just as you apply the sweep.

In training we keep hold of our opponents arm if we are not using mats, so they can fall safely.

Downward Strike - Defence 3

This is a simple defence that uses a low turning kick to destroy the attackers leg.

1a, 1b, 1c & 1d. As the attacker comes forwards to execute the downward strike (or even if there is no step into it), side step and simultaneously execute a low turning kick to the front of the attackers thigh, using your shin as the striking part of the leg.

2. Follow up with a right cross (or left cross if reversed)

Notes: *As this kick attacks the thigh muscle, not much conditioning work is required for the defenders shin.* Also, if you misjudge things, you can always replace the low turning kick for a knee strike and follow up with an elbow strike.

Downward Strike - Defence 4

Once again we are going to use the forearm rising block first found in Dan-Gun tul transitioning into a shoulder throw.

1a, 1b & 1c. As the attacker attempts their downward strike, execute a basic forearm rising block to intercept it.

1c, 2a & 2b. Immediately as the block makes contact, step in towards your opponent, hooking your opposite arm underneath their armpit whilst pivoting 180 degrees. At the same time rotate your previous rising block to the outside and grab your opponents other arm. Lower your centre of gravity by dropping down a bit whilst pulling on the grabbed arm.

3a & 3b. Straighten your legs as you pull the opponent upwards and forwards, executing the shoulder throw.

4. If you have maintained your grip on the opponents arm as they landed, you should be able to use your knee to break the opponents elbow joint, simply by pivoting

into it, whilst pulling their arm straight (although its likely to be pretty straight already following the throw). Alternatively, you can pull the arm sharply across your knee instead.

Defences Against Pushes And Shoves

A push is often a precursor to something more sinister and is basically a hard shove with the attackers palm, using either one or both hands, with the intent to either turn you or unbalance you, perhaps knocking you down.

In training students should try not to pre-empt the push if they know its coming, by moving to early. As well as practicing to slip them, they should also learn what to do after the actual contact has been made, such as when they are travelling backwards or turning whilst unbalanced. To do this, we usually stand in a parallel stance, with no fence or other guard in place.

Double Push - Defence 1

For this defence we use the outer forearm wedging block and front snap kick combination from Do-San tul.

1a, 1b, 1c & 1d. As the attacker shoves you backwards, bring your arms up in the chamber position for the wedging block and execute the block, using the 'closed fists' part of the block as a grab onto the attackers arms, in order to help stabilise yourself and avoid being pushed too far backwards.

2. As soon as your stabilised, immediately counter attack with a front snap kick, either to the attackers body or groin, whilst maintaining your grip on the attackers arms. Because you are using the attackers own arms to stabilise you, you do not have to wait until you come to a full stop before counter attacking, making your counter attack much quicker to deliver.

Double Push - Defence 2

For this defence, we work on the fact that we didn't react quickly enough to defend against the double push and are shoved forcefully backwards. To stabilise ourselves quickly, as we are going backwards we turn into a sitting or L stance, then quickly counter attack with a front leg side piercing kick before the attacker can follow up.

1a, 1b & 1c. As we are pushed forcefully backwards, try and turn into an L-stance or a sitting stance so we regain our balance quickly.

2a & 2b. As we went backwards, away from the attacker, we are at a good distance to execute a side piercing kick, especially if the attacker is intent on following up himself. We execute the side piercing kick off the front leg for speed, thrusting it out sharply like a boxers jab.

Double Push - Defence 3

This defence requires slightly quicker reflexes than the others, as you need to side step and parry, before using a palm hooking block from Yul-Gok tul to capitalize on the attackers momentum.

1a & 1b. As the attacker attempts their double push, side step and use your outside hand to keep the attackers arms in the same direction by parrying them with your palm.

 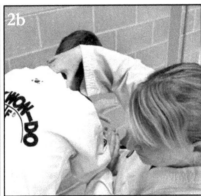 

2a, 2b & 2c. As the attacker starts to pass you, use your palm hooking block by wrapping it around the back of the opponents head and scooping it backwards in the same direction the attacker is already travelling, throwing them off-balance and (hopefully) to the floor via their own momentum. Even if they don't go down, it still puts you in a good position, behind the attacker, so you can apply a choke technique.

Double Push - Defence 4

This final defence takes into account not only the double push, but the fact that you have actually been knocked down by it.

1a & 1b. We are pushed over by the attackers double push attack.

2. Instead of stumbling backwards, trying to regain our balance, giving the attacker more time to move in and follow up, we relax and go with the flow and allow ourselves to fall directly backwards, putting our hands out to break our fall.

3. As soon as we make contact with the ground, we flick out our front snap kick, catching the attacker before they can execute a follow up technique of their own.

Single Push - Defence 1

For this defence we use the palm pushing block from Hwa-Rang tul.

1a, 1b, 1c & 1d. As the attacker attempts to shove you, side step and execute a palm pushing block to the attackers arm. Hit the arm as high up as you can, as the aim here isn't just to redirect the attackers arm, but to turn their upper body.

2. As the attacker is turned, move in behind them, placing your lead arm in front of their neck.

3a & 3b. Grab the arm you just placed in front and pull it tightly to your body and execute a rear naked choke.

Single Push - Defence 2

For this defence we use the momentum of the attackers push to add power to our counter-strike.

1a, 1b & 1c. As the attacker shoves you, relax and twist your shoulders, simply using the opposite arm (to where the push is), to strike with a right (or left) cross. If the push is in the centre of your chest, simply relax and twist your upper body to 'slip' the push a bit, counter-attacking in the same way.

Single Push - Defence 3

This defence is similar to the previous one, but is ideal if the push is more forceful, causing you to step back slightly or turn a lot more. As before, it uses the momentum from the attackers push to add power to our counter-strike, by using the motions first found in Do-San tul.

1a, 1b & 1c. As the attacker shoves you, relax your upper body and try to take it on one side if possible. If its centred, just relax and twist into it.

2. Spin around and throw your elbow up to catch your opponent on the spin.

3a & 3b. Depending on your distance, you can also counter-strike with a forearm strike or a backfist strike

Single Push - Defence 4

This defence relies on fast reactions, but if you have a fence up, then your lead hand will already be in a good position to execute this defence and counter-strike.

1a & 1b. As the attacker attempts to shove you, use your lead hand to parry the push. It doesn't have to be powerful, just enough to take it off course.

2. Immediately react off your parry and use the same hand to hit your opponent with a backfist strike. This will likely be a stunning blow, so use the opportunity to follow up with other techniques.

Defences Against Elbow Strikes

Elbow strikes are devastatingly effective techniques and being hit with one can end a situation instantly. Whilst rear, side and downward elbow strikes are mostly used in counter attacks or as in-fighting techniques, the front elbow and its close cousin the turning elbow strike, are often used as attacking techniques.

On the plus side, to execute a front or turning elbow effectively, the attacker must be at quite a close range and in a real situation, proper use of the fence will negate this range becoming a reality. On the down side, should the attacker get into the range to release a front or turning elbow strike, the defender will have very little reaction time to defend against it. So this section takes this minimal reaction time into account in its defences against them. All the defence techniques shown here can be used against both a front elbow strike and a turning elbow strike (sometimes referred to a 'cutting' elbow).

Front Or Turning Elbow Strike - Defence 1

With minimal reaction time, we look to cover and absorb the blow before going with the flow to execute our counter attack.

1a, 1b & 1c. As the attacker tries to hit you with their elbow, raise your shoulder as high as you can, dropping your head down behind your shoulder for cover whilst turning away from the impact, taking the elbow strike on your shoulder. Tense your jaw and bring your rear hand up for extra protection.

2a, 2b & 2c. Use the flow of the attack and keep spinning (180 degrees) and land an elbow strike of your own (a spinning elbow strike).

3. From there, you can follow up with punches if need be.

Front Or Turning Elbow Strike - Defence 2

For this defence, if we are able to get our hands up in time, we use the outer forearm parallel block, followed by the one leg stance combination that we find in Juche tul.

1a & 1b. As the attacker throws their elbow strike at you, bring up both arms in front and take the blow on your outer forearms, just like the outer forearm parallel block from Juche tul. However, due to reaction time, it is best to simply bring the arms straight up, as opposed to chambering them first, which would mean the block not working at all!

2a, 2b & 2c. Without removing your arms, immediately execute the one leg stance, using it as a knee strike. You can target your opponents stomach (2a), groin (2b) or use a turning knee instead to attack his ribs or thigh (2c).

Front Or Turning Elbow Strike - Defence 3

For this defence we are going to avoid the elbow strike altogether, dropping down (like in Choong-Jang tul), but instead of executing the high punch, we use a simple low outer forearm block as a takedown technique.

1a & 1b. As the attacker throws their elbow strike, drop straight down onto one knee and immediately grab the attackers leg, behind their heel or calf, placing your other arm above their knee, on their thigh.

2a & 2b. Pull their leg forwards with your lower hand, whilst pressing down firmly on their thigh with your other forearm. Keep going until they fall backwards.

If they are able to retain their b a l a n c e s o m e h o w , simply stand up whilst still holding their leg and throw it up and forwards to unbalance them.

3. Once the attacker is on the floor, counter attack with a punch to the groin, then quickly stand up and escape.

Front Or Turning Elbow Strike - Defence 4

Again, for this defence we are going to avoid the elbow strike altogether and drop down. It's a good defence if your at very close range and involves using a side break fall motion to take down the attacker.

1a & 1b. As the attacker throws their elbow strike, drop straight down, trying to place your arm to the outside of the attackers leg (this isn't essential, but helps).

2a & 2b. Roll directly into the attackers thigh with your side, hooking their leg with your arm if possible.

3a & 3b. As the attackers leg is locked, they will lose balance and falls backwards, whereby you continue your roll and use your elbow to strike the attacker.

Taking A Punch

Sometimes things escalate so fast its not always possible to defend properly against a punch and you simply get hit! However, even when hit, you can respond immediately with a counter attack, instinctively.

Of course, punches hurt, but your face can take them a lot better if your jaw is tensed as the moment of impact.

Taking A Punch - Defence 1

Technically, this is less of a defence and more of a response, however it's a good response to learn so its executed automatically if you are hit.

1a, 1b & 1c. As you are hit with the attackers punch, go with the flow of it (which will take some of the force away from it as well), rather than trying to 'take it' full on, allow it to spin you around. If it's a straight punch, spin as well!

2a, 2b & 2c. As you spin, raise your arms and use the continued momentum to strike the attacker with a spinning elbow - don't stop and strike, but spin right through for a greater impact.

Note: *It is best to practice this with a lighter punch from a padded training partner, so they can hit you and then hold their gloved hands up to take the spinning elbow strike. Alternatively, use focus pads.*

Taking A Punch - Defence 2

This is a technique I use a lot, it is part block and part 'taking the shot' and its called a 'triangle block'. It can be used for any incoming punch, a slap or similar attack. It's a way of reacting to something quickly, as you basically cover and take some of the power out of the shot and its very quick (and natural) to execute from a fence position.

To perform it, you make a triangle shape with your arm, bringing your hand up to your head, covering but not cupping your ear and in this way, you cover your jaw, your ear, your head, your throat and your cheek from the incoming blow. At the same time you execute the block, you also turn away from the blow as well

1a, 1b & 1c. As the punch is thrown towards your head, bring you hand and arm to the 'triangle block' position (as described above), turning your upper body off-line or away from the direction of the strike.

2. As soon as you have taken the shot, counter-attack by striking with your opposite hand.

Taking A Punch - Defence 3

This is a counter-attack for a punch that has hit hard and knocks you backwards.

1a & 1b. As the attacker lands their punch and knocks you backwards, go with the flow of the punch to steal some of the power from it.

2a & 2b. With the momentary shock from the punch, step backwards, away from the punch, to allow a bit of recovery time, to regain your balance and to nullify any immediate follow up punches from the attacker, thus forcing them to move forwards to strike you again.

3a & 3b. As soon as you have regained some balance, kick out with a back piercing kick in the direction of the attacker.

In most cases, we do not have to look prior to kicking out at the attacker, as we know its in the opposite direction to which we have stepped.

The back piercing kick is an ideal counter-attack as it can connect with the attacker, no matter how far they have stepped forwards, meaning it doesn't have to 'lock out' like a standard back piercing kick in training, as it can cause a hard impact even with the knee bent. Also, the height doesn't matter so much, as we can hit the opponent in their gut, their thigh or their knee and even if it doesn't hit, it will force the attacker to pause, allowing us more recovery time (*see section; Keeping An Aggressive Opponent At Bay*) in preparation for the ensuing 'fight' . Finally, it allows us to keep our hands up, as if the back piercing kick misses, we need to cover our head from repeated blows from the attacker.

Important Tips For Taking A Punch
No one likes to take a punch to the head, that is for sure, but you can try to minimise the damage it does.

1. Always try to close your mouth tightly and tense your jaw. This can mean the difference between 'taking it' and it hurting (obviously) and getting knocked out and/or losing a few teeth.

2. Turn your head away (slightly) from the punch if possible. This steals some of the power from the punch and may even make it hit a less vulnerable point than your jaw bone (the 'standard' target).

3. As well as turning your head slightly, tuck your jaw into your shoulder, as this covers the jaw line.

4. If you do see a punch coming and have enough time to react, move sharply backwards, as this can take a lot of power from the punch, even if it lands.

5. Take your hits in class, don't wait until its for real, so you know what it feels like and know you can recover quickly from it. This doesn't mean you have to ask someone to punch you in class, simply that, when sparring and you get hit, learn to take it and carry on (unless you are bleeding or properly injured of course).

6. Understand that a bone to bone punch (meaning your opponents knuckles to your jaw bone) can do a lot more damage than taking one with a pair of sparring gloves on. Get a training partner to 'very lightly', tap your (clenched) jaw with their knuckles to feel the effect on your head/brain.

Chapter 4
Defences Against Kicks

Defences Against Kicks

A kick is really any techniques where the attacker tries to strike you by using their legs, which includes knee strikes. Where as most Taekwon-Do students are used to evading, blocking and counter-attacking against middle and high section kicks, they are not so well versed against low section kicks or knee strikes.

Also, its important to remember that the way a person kicks is usually different between a trained fighter and a non-trained fighter and thus the angles of attack are different. For example, a student of Taekwon-Do will execute a front (snap) kick, by raising his knee first, then thrusting forwards, where as a non-trained attacker will often do it 'football' style, bringing it up and forwards at the same time in an arc. Attacking tools can vary as well, a Taekwon-Do student would execute the front kick with the ball of the foot, where-as a non-martial artist may use the toes, instep or the shin.

But, it is just as important not to discount more martial art style kicks, as many more people practice martial arts these days and thus some aggressors are likely to have some kicking skills. In this section, we explore defences for the various types of kicks from both trained and non-trained aggressors.

'Football' Style Front Kick - Defence 1

For this defence, we use the circular block from Won-Hyo tul.

1a, 1b & 1c. As the attacker starts to swing the kick towards you, move into it slightly and drop your body downwards, starting to execute the circular block as you do so.

2a, 2b, 2c & 2d. Meet the kick before it reaches its full arc of

power, by using the 'non' blocking arm to shield yourself and intercept the kick, by placing it across the top of the kicking leg (trying to intercept it closer to your elbow

joint, where the arm is thicker), whilst your actual blocking arms intercepts it on the side and wraps around it in the circular motion, trapping the attackers leg between your two arms.

Note: *It is a good idea to dip a bit lower than you do in the patterns so as to intercept the actual kick earlier in its trajectory.*

- From this point you are in control as you have the attacker at a major disadvantage as he is balanced on one leg, which presents a lot of options.

3a, 3b & 3c. Option 1 is to follow the moves as they appear in the pattern, literally throwing the kick off to the side (which turns the attacker), following up with a front snap kick of your own to the coccyx, with the reverse punch follow up. This is also the follow up you can use if you didn't manage to 'trap' the actual kick and simply blocked it anyway - of course, attack to which ever area presents itself, depending on how the attacker landed.

4. If you did trap the kick successfully, you can use

your own body to lock it in place, trapping the attackers foot between your blocking arm and your own body (one of the reasons we off-turn our shoulders when executing the circular block in patterns practice.). From here you have good control still and you can again, follow up as in the pattern itself, by executing a front snap kick (or a front rising kick) to the attackers groin.

- The more advanced student can use the application for the twin palm downward block, as detailed in Ch'ang Hon Taekwon-do Hae Sul; vol 2.

'Football' Style Front Kick - Defence 2

For this defence, we use a forearm or reverse knifehand low inward block, as found in Eui-Am tul, to deflect the kick, whilst using our momentum to counter-attack.

1a, 1b & 1c. As the attacker starts to swing the kick towards you, turn your body sideways and push your knee outwards. We do this to protect our groin (by taking it out of the line of attack), but also in the hope of deflecting the kick with our shin, by meeting it side on.

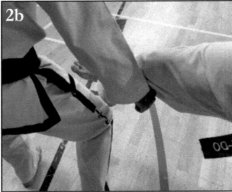

2a & 2b. As well as turning and extending our shin, we also execute the inward block. Between the shin and the arm, this creates a defensive line in front of our body in the hope that at some point along it, it will meet and intercept the kick., whether that is quite low (our shin) or travels further and thus higher (our forearm).

3a & 3b. With either the shin or our forearm we are looking to parry the kick out

to the side and we use our momentum from the turn and continue through executing a back piercing kick before the attacker recovers and re-adjusts.

'Football' Style Front Kick - Defence 3

This defence requires some fast reflexes as it uses the legs instead of the arms to defend against the attack, using a variation of the low twisting kick first seen in Ge-Baek tul.

1a, 1b, 1c & 1d. As the attacker starts to swing the kick towards you execute an oblique kick (variation of the twisting kick) by bringing your leg forward to meet the incoming kick - turning your foot outwards as you do so as in this way, you have a much larger area to intercept the incoming kick.

2a, 2b, 2c & 2d. At soon as the attackers kick is intercepted, they will be momentarily off-balance and you have two choices, depending on your skill level and your own level of balance at that point.

The first option is to place your foot back down and counter-attack by kicking with the other leg, in this case a turning kick. (pictures 2a & 2b).

The second option is to rebound straight off your block and counter attack with the same leg (pictures 2c & 2d).

3a & 3b. Follow up on your counter kicks with some straight punches.

'Football' Style Front Kick - Defence 4

This defence is useful if the kick is at a slightly longer range and can also be used against a martial arts style front kick, as it uses the X-fist pressing block that we first see in Toi-Gye tul, but also the counter attack is the following move to the X-fist pressing block, that is found in the 2nd degree pattern Choong-Jang tul.

1a, 1b & 1c. As the attackers kick travels towards you, execute the X-fist pressing block to intercept the kick. There is no need for a big 'chamber' here, as simply crossing your arms will do the job well.

2. As soon as you intercept the kick, grab it with both hands.

3a & 3b. Moving the attackers leg to the side, counter attack by executing a knee kick to the femoral artery, which is located on the attackers inside thigh. An alternative target would be the attackers groin, if you are too close.

*3b Reversed - showing both target areas
- inside thigh and groin*

Defences Against Circular Kicks

A circular kick is most often known as a turning kick or a round house kick in Taekwon-Do and other martial arts and is any kick that travels in a circular motion. Whilst Taekwon-Do students are often fairly well versed at dodging or parrying middle and high circular kicks, they are often not as comfortable in low circular kick defences or even following up a middle or high circular kick attack, with a viable defence, that doesn't involve allowing the opponents to place their kicking leg down.

Low Circular Kick - Defence 1

Taking a full power low circular kick to the side of your knee or your thigh is no fun at all and will seriously inhibit your ability to fight back against your attacker effectively, so we are going to use the one leg stance, that we first see in Po-Eun tul, to block the attack, giving us space to counter-attack.

1a, 1b & 1c. Immediately raise your leg to the one leg stance position as soon as the attacker launches their kick towards your knee or thigh - do not turn towards the kick, as unless you have some good shin conditioning, a shin block will hurt a lot!

1c Note. When you raise your knee, ensure you bring your foot up as well and don't leave your toes pointing towards the floor. This tenses your calf muscle, which will absorb some of the blow.

2. After taking the kick, counter-strike as you drop your foot back to the ground.

Low Circular Kick - Defence 2

This is a variation on the last defence and is ideal if you are not in a solid position to bear the brunt of the kick or don't wish to take the full force of the kick.

1a, 1b & 1c. As the low kick is launched, raise your knee to the one leg stance position, as per the previous defence.

2. Instead of taking the force of the attackers kick full on, allow it to knock your leg to the side - which is actually starting your counter strike for you. It also means the impact will be lessened.

3a, 3b & 3c. Utilizing the spinning motion, step down and execute a back piercing kick with your other leg.

Low Circular Kick - Defence 3

Once again, this defence involves raising the knee, however this time, the idea is to avoid the attackers kick altogether and thus is a good defence for the student who is reasonably flexible or against a low kick executed further away or which is aimed a bit lower.

1a & 1b. As the opponent attempts to low kick you, raise your knee as high as you can, with the intent of stepping over the kick.

2a & 2b. Bring your leg over the kick allowing the attackers own momentum to turn them.

3a & 3b. Step down and immediately counter attack with a low turning kick of your own to the back of the attackers thigh or knee joint.

Note: If the attacker hasn't over-rotated, their outside thigh may be exposed for the counter-attack, but if they have (as per the pictures) your own low kick counter will be unlikely to take them out and will simply either turn them further or bend them,

so their head is lower.

4a or 4b. Depending on the position of your attacker at this point, follow up with a strike (4a) or, if they have turned enough, you can move in and execute a choke (4b).

Low Circular Kick - Defence 4

This is less of a defence and more of a damage limitation technique to be used if your reactions were not fast enough to move your front leg for a counter or block, taking the kick to the back of the thigh or knee, rather than the side of the thigh (where the main pressure point is) or the side of the knee.

1a, 1b & 1c. As the low turning kick is thrown towards you, turn your leg away from the kick, so it doesn't strike the side of your thigh or knee, but rather the back of your thigh or knee. This will still hurt, but as the knee flexes, it will take away some of the impact, as well as removing the pressure point target in your thigh (which can destroy your leg altogether).

2. Immediately twist back in and strike the opponent as they regain balance following the kick.

Mid/High Circular Kick - Defence 1

For this defence, we take the kick on our arm, trap it and perform a sweep to take the opponent down.

1a, 1b & 1c. As the kick travels towards you, raise your shoulder to protect your jaw and take the kick on your upper arm. Use a palm block with your opposite arm to help defend should the kick actually travel higher than your shoulders, though you can nullify this by stepping in slightly. Also, keep your arm bent in case you are hit on the elbow joint!

2a & 2b. As soon as the kick makes contact, hook your forearm around the attackers leg and grab hold of their clothing.

3. Bring your rear leg forwards, taking it behind the attackers supporting leg.

4a, 4b, 4c & 4d. Sweep your leg backwards, hitting the opponents calf muscle with your own, whilst pushing in the opposite direction with your gripped hand. Alternatively, step your foot down next to the opponents and push them to trip them over your leg (4b). This will take away their supporting leg, sending them crashing into the floor.

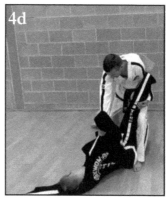

For training, try to keep a grip on your partner in order to soften their landing a bit, in a real attack scenario, you can choose whether to let go or not!

Mid/High Circular Kick - Defence 2

For this defence, we take the kick on our arm, counter with a knee kick then use a twin palm downward block, that we first see in Eui-Am tul, to take the opponent down.

1a & 1b. As the opponent kicks, take the kick on your upper arm, looping it around the attackers leg.

2. Step forwards so your opposite palm is on top of the attackers knee joint.

3a or 3b. Quickly counter attack with a knee kick to the attackers groin or inner thigh (which will help make them turn away). Alternatively, you can use a straight downward elbow to the side of the attackers knee joint.

4a, 4b & 4c. As they turn, press down on the back (and/or side) of the attackers knee joint with your front hand. You can accentuate this by raising the end of the attackers leg, by raising your body (the rear foot stance in the pattern). Raising it will also help turn the attackers leg to expose the back of their knee.

5a & 5b. Keep pressing down until the attacker goes to the floor.

Mid/High Circular Kick - Defence 3

For this defence, we use a couple of techniques from Dan-Gun tul, that all 8th kup students learn. They work together to firstly trap the kick and then execute a takedown.

1a, 1b & 1c. As the opponent kicks, move in and turn towards the kick, whilst starting to execute the chamber position for a knifehand guarding block, ensuring your rear hand (the side of the kick) is kept lower than the kick and your front

hand is up, just in case you misjudge the height of the kick.

Moving in towards the attacker will allow you to nullify a high kick to your head, as you will intercept it at a lower point along the attackers leg.

2a & 2b. As you feel the attackers kick hit your bicep, immediately execute your knifehand guarding block, trapping the attackers leg with your rear hand. You can use your front hand as a strike to the attackers head if your are close enough, or change it to grip their shoulder for further control or even use it to defend against a hand strike from the attacker if needed (2b).

3a & 3b. With the attackers leg under our control, we simply follow the pattern sequence that we have practiced so many times solo and step forwards whilst executing a high forefist punch. Our forward body momentum combined with our arm travelling upwards, pushes the opponents leg further upwards and beyond their point of balance, causing them to get thrown over.

Note: *When practicing this in class, it is a good idea to execute the 2nd part slowly and hold onto your opponents dobok as you do so, to help them fall a bit more slowly.* **Executing this at full speed is extremely dangerous!**

Mid/High Circular Kick - Defence 4

You will have already seen this technique in the hand attacks section, as its very universal in its use. This time we are using the triangle block to cover and take a high turning kick attack.

As the the target of a circular kick is often unclear, the defence is put up just in case it is a high kick, but if the kick is performed lower, at mid level, you may get a kick in the ribs, though if you keep the triangle block tight, some of the kicks power will be absorbed into your arm.

1a, 1b & 1c. As the kick comes in, bring your hand up to the triangle block position, placing your hand on your head to cover your face, whilst turning away from the attack slightly.

Once you have taken the kick, immediately counter attack, preferably before the opponent regains full stability before they put their kicking leg down.

Defences Against Side Kicks

In the main, middle or high side kicks shouldn't prove too much of an issue for a student who has trained regularly for some time, as good footwork can be used to avoid them, however, low side kicks (to the knee, shin or thigh) can be a problem, as they are not allowed in much of Taekwon-Do standard training, especially sparring, so can unexpectedly catch the student out. A low side kick is very capable of damaging your front leg if it locks it straight and, because its low and quick, fairly hard to avoid, so some of these defences rely on quick reactions.

Low Side Kick - Defence 1

This defence is useful, as it requires minimal reaction time. It basically uses a bending ready stance A to absorb the kick.

1a, 1b, 1c & 1d. As your opponent starts to chamber and throw their low side piercing kick, quickly raise your front knee up in a bent position. If the kick was aimed at the knee, this brings the target higher, causing the kick to strike lower, hitting your shin instead of your knee.

As the kick hits your shin allow your lower leg to hinge at the knee and bend backwards, removing some of the power from the kick as well as forcing the opponent to extend it fully.

2a & 2b. As the opponent places their kicking foot back to the ground, before they regain their

composure, drop your raised foot back down (and thus your weight) and as you do so, use the momentum to strike the opponent.

As a bonus, if the kick was actually aimed higher, your action of raising the leg, can function as a knee jam instead.

Low Side Kick - Defence 2

Ironically, this defence comes straight out of the **tournament sparring playbook, yet is a good response when reaction time is limited to almost nil!** The main thing is, in the minimal time you have, to **protect your knee joint from damage.**

1a & 1b. As the low side kick is thrown, immediately bend your front knee and tense it in readiness for the incoming kick.

Being bent and tense will limit the damage providing more protection for the knee joint.

2a. & 2b. As the kick strikes you and whilst the opponent is balanced on one leg, lean forwards and throw a counter-strike at the opponents face, following up with other techniques whilst they are stunned.

Low Side Kick - Defence 3

A bit of footwork, coupled with decent reflexes can work well when having to defend against low level kicks, which again, are attributes you can gain through standard free sparring.

1a, 1b & 1c. As the opponent throws thir low side kick, shuffle or step backwards, so you are just out of range of the kick.

2a, 2b or 2c. Before the opponent regains their posture, dart forward with a skip whilst executing a low turning kick to their solar plexus or groin.

Low Side Kick - Defence 4

This defence uses sidestepping to avoid the kick, prior to counter-attacking.

1a, 1b & 1c. As the low side kick is thrown towards you, shuffle back slightly whilst side stepping to avoid the kick.

2. Immediately move back in, now at a slight angle, to the outside and counter attack your opponent using hand strikes.

Mid/High Side Kick - Defence 1

If the kick is thrown off the front leg, we have minimum reaction time, so use an outer forearm parallel block, that we find in Juche tul, to take the brunt of the kick

1a & 1b. As the kick is thrown, bring your forearms together in front of you, drop your chin and take the blow on your arms. Moving forwards, into the kick will also dissipate some of its power.

2a & 2b. Try and counter-attack before or as the opponent puts their kicking leg back down on the floor, overwhelming them with straight punches.

Mid/High Side Kick - Defence 2

For this defence, if you have time to react, you are going to side step and hook the kick with your arm prior to counter-attacking.

1a, 1b & 1c. As the attacker throws the kick, side step to the outside (and forwards if possible), keeping your closest arm low, whilst bringing your opposite arm/hand up to protect your head.

2. As the kick is dodged and becomes level with your arm, quickly hook your arm up and around the opponents leg.

3a & 3b. While keeping the opponents leg held tightly, quickly counter attack with a kick of your own, such as a low kick to the opponents knee (3a) or the knee kick to their groin (3b).

4a & 4b. If your counter kick hasn't already finished the opponent, you can continue by striking the side of the opponents grabbed leg, on the knee joint, with a downward elbow strike. Strike down hard and continue by pressing the point of your elbow into the opponents knee joint, which will cause them to drop to the

ground to alleviate the pain.

Mid/High Side Kick - Defence 3

This defence requires a little bit of flexibility, but not so much that the average student cannot do it! It basically uses a knee kick, to check and parry the opponents side kick.

1a, 1b, 1c & 1d. As the attacker throws their kick, raise your knee up in a slightly arcing motion, intercepting the kick with the side of your shin. The slight arcing motion will cause the attackers leg to be knocked off course. ***Note:*** *Ensure you keep*

your guard up as well, in case the kick is higher than expected.

2a, 2b & 2c. With the opponent off balance and likely turned (depending on how hard your parry was), move in quickly and apply a rear naked choke. Alternatively, if not turned enough, follow up with hand strikes.

Mid/High Side Kick - Defence 4

To defend against this technique, we use a similar technique to the one we find in Moon-Moo tul (the palm downward block), however instead of slipping our front foot, we take a full step backwards.

1a & 1b. As the attacker throws out their side kick, step backwards a full stride to take you out of range of the kick.

2a & 2b. Along with stepping backwards, execute a palm downward block to the side of the attackers leg, knocking it downwards towards the floor.

Do not step back so your rear foot is flat on the floor, just step back onto the ball of your foot so that you can instantly 'spring' forwards again with

your counter attack.

3a, 3b & 3c. As soon as you have b l o c k e d t h e attackers kick, before they have a chance to regain their composure, immediately spring forwards with your rear leg with a low turning kick of your own, counter attacking either the attackers groin (3b) or the attackers thigh (3c), depending on your distance.

Mid/High Side Kick - *Notes*

1. One thing to remember when defending against side kicks, is that although they are usually executed off the front leg of the attacker, often the attacker will also incorporate a skip, shuffle or slide as they execute it, which you need to take into account if your defence involves moving backwards to avoid the kick.

2. A non-trained person will often have less of a chambering motion, than a standard, trained student, meaning they will bring their leg to the final side kick position in an almost 'straight up and out' motion, which has less power, but also leaves the defender with less reaction time. On the plus side, the opponents balance will be impaired much easier by the trained student,.

Jamming Mid/High Side Kicks 1

If you have quick reactions, you can actually jam a lot of middle or high kicks as they are being executed. As well as side and turning kicks, this defence also works well with front leg hooking kicks, reverse turning kicks, back piercing kicks and any other kick that doesn't involve a 'straight in front' type of chamber, such as a front snap kick, though the effect would still be similar, though you would hit the leg of the attacker, not the hip as shown here.

1a, 1b, 1c & 1d. As the attacker starts to chamber their kick (or starts spinning for a reverse turning kick), immediately dart forwards, aiming to hit the opponent's hip with your own.

Move in fast and hard and smash the side of your hip into the opponent who, as they are on one leg, will either be knocked over or at the very least knocked off balance.

2a, 2b & 2c. If they are knocked to the floor you can run or follow up with stamping kicks or other downward attacks, but if they are just unbalanced, continue using your forward momentum and execute a side piercing kick or, as shown here, a back piercing kick.

Jamming Mid/High Side Kicks 2

Depending on your reaction times, you can actually use the first part of a side piercing kick chamber, to jam an incoming side piercing kick, using your knee.

1a, 1b & 1c. As the opponent raises their leg to execute their side piercing kick, bring your own knee straight up in front of you to intercept and jam the opponents incoming kick before it reaches its full extension. As long as you raise your knee quickly, to your centre, then you should intercept their kick.

2a, 2b & 2c. Whilst the opponents is unbalanced, step your front knee down and spring off the back foot, executing a low turning kick to the attackers thigh or knee.

3. Follow up your low turning kick with hand strikes.

Spinning Sweep Against A Mid/High Side Kick

This is a fairly dangerous technique to execute, as it involves dropping onto the floor, in front of your opponent which, if you get it wrong, leaves you in a vulnerable position, however, if you get it right, its devastating. And its not to hard to learn!

1a & 1b. As the attacker starts to kick, drop down towards the ground and start to spin. This motion takes your body and head away from the kick, placing them away from the immediate threat.

2a & 2b. Drop onto your knee, placing a hand on the floor for balance and keep spinning. As you continue to spin round, extend your leg aiming to hit the attackers calf muscle, just above their ankle. Too high and your likely to simply cause them to buckle at the knee, but not drop!

3a & 3b. Aim to not only hit the attackers leg, but go right through it, taking them down as you do so. Then quickly get to your feet and finish off if needed.

Note: You can practice the spinning sweep in isolation by using a kick shield placed on the floor.

Also, in the dojang, ensure you practice this technique on mats and if your partner isn't competent in rear breakfalls, then do not follow through with the sweep, but simply stop when you hit the calf muscle, to avoid injury.

This technique can also be employed against other middle or high kick attacks, such as turning kicks, reverse turning kicks and even back piercing kicks, just remember to spin the right way; switch your stance when you drop down if need be, as you need to attack the back of the opponents leg.

Defences Against Knee Kicks

Knee kicks (or knee strikes) are very hard to defend against, as they are usually employed at close range, whilst grappling with an opponent., so our focus is on upper body defence, so when an opponent strikes with their knee, the usual natural reaction is to bring our arms down to cover against it, which leaves us open up top! However, there are some defences that can be employed and these are detailed here.

Knee Kick - Defence 1

In Taekwon-Do there is a stance that you will not see performed in any of the patterns which is called 'Crouched Stance', it is similar to a 'Diagonal Stance' but the knees are bent inwards. In this defence we use a position similar to crouched stance, but also a natural flinch reflex, which is to protect the groin!

1a, 1b & 1c. Using natural instinct or fast reflexes, you catch the opponents knee kick, by bringing your own knees together, trapping the opponents knee between your own.

2. Keeping your knees tight together, sharply pivot 90 degree's. You can pivot either way, but I find turning into the inside of the opponent's leg has the effect of unbalancing them as you apply pressure to either their inside knee or inner thigh, whereby you can use their shoulders to accentuate their unbalancing.

Close up of the knee trap and twist

Knee Kick - Defence 2

If you are lucky enough to see a knee coming, you can defend and counter attack using the x-fist pressing block and twin vertical fist punch from Toi-Gye tul.

1a & 1b. Block the opponents knee kick using an x-fist pressing block.

2a & 2b. As soon as the opponents knee hits your block, grab hold of their knee with both hands and pull it upwards to disrupt their balance.

3. If you have a good grip on the knee (and are fairly strong) you can maintain your grip and with the knee pulled high, throw it backwards using the twin vertical fist punch motion.

Alternatively, as its likely your grip won't be that secure, as you pull up the opponents knee, as they start to lose balance, release your grip and use the twin vertical fist punch motion to push them backwards.

Chapter 5
Defences Against Grabs

Precursor Techniques

A 'precursor technique' is a technique that precedes the main technique, in order to make it work more effectively. It is designed to alter the thought process of the opponent for a split second, for example, taking their mind away from a grab (so its easier to manipulate) by moving it to a pain point we have caused in their leg. The effects will usually only last for a split second, but in self defence a split second is a long time and allows us to do what's needed.

A precursor technique is very useful for creating wiggle room when trapped in a bear hug or a rear choke, allowing you some room to manoeuvre. They are also useful when attempting to apply a locking technique, and sometimes before attempting a throwing technique.

Tomasz, who is demonstrating with me in these photo's is about 6' 5" tall, weighs about 90kg and is immensely strong, the strongest student in class in fact. It is extremely unlikely that once he has established a solid grip on me (in this case a single lapel grab) and tensed his fist and arm, that I would simply be able to grab his wrist and twist it to the desired position to obtain a wrist lock.

So what I do is take his thought process away from his grip temporarily and I do this by using an oblique kick to his shin. This causes his brain to recognise and react to the pain, thus moving his thought process away from the grip he has, which in turn, allows me to apply my wrist lock, which I execute almost simultaneously to the oblique kick, locking his wrist, then following up with a front snap kick of my own.

Example Precursor Techniques

Oblique Kick to Shin

This is really the only front facing technique I use, as it works well due to high/low line of sight, meaning the attacker doesn't see it coming as their attacks are concentrated on the upper body and even if they do see it, as it comes almost straight forwards, in a straight line, reacting to it is almost impossible due to its speed of execution.

Whilst you could use a front snap kick, with an oblique kick, its much easier to hit the target, even without looking, as you turn your foot outwards, giving you a greater area to strike with. A stamp to the opponents knee would cause greater damage, but as you have to raise your foot to execute such a technique, it is telegraphed much more and thus allows the opponent to react which isn't the response we want.

This is used mostly prior to attempting wrist or arm locks, lapel grab releases, or stepping in to execute a throwing technique.

The following precursor techniques are used when defending against rear attacks such as bear hugs and rear chokes, prior to executing a throw (if grabbed from the rear) or to create room to manoeuvre, so you can escape or turn.

Foot Stamp

Simply raise your foot then stamp on the top of the opponents foot with your heel. It works great in bare feet, due to the small bones in the attackers foot being exposed and would also work well if wearing hard shoes (with a solid heel) or high heels.

If the initial stamp doesn't achieve the required response, either keep repeating it or grind your heel into the attackers foot.

For training we usually stamp next to our partner foot as they know what it represents and thus loosen their grip accordingly.

Back Snap Kick

Simply flick your foot back and upwards to execute, aiming for the attackers groin.

Some find this a bit more difficult than other techniques, but you can use your own body to calculate where the attackers groin is, as usually an opponents legs will be directly behind your own, so their centre and groin will be in direct relation to yours, just further back.

For training, don't kick your partner in the groin by keeping the kick a little lower, or kick the inside of their thigh instead, allowing them to react as they would in a real situation.

Rear Headbutt

For a rear headbutt, there is no need to wind it up first by bringing your head forwards, before butting backwards, as this would allow the opponent to react as you telegraph the technique. Instead, simply whip your head backwards onto the opponents face.

In training, if a rear headbutt is being practiced, ensure your partner has their face turned away and head moved to the side so they don't get hit with it. As with other techniques, your training partner should respond as they would in a real situation.

Shin Drag

Ideal if you are wearing hard shoes. Raise your foot and move (or kick) it back into the opponents shin, so the side of your foot is touching it, then, keeping hard contact with the opponents shin, dragging it downwards along their shin bone.

In training, with bare feet, this doesn't hurt that much, so is safe to execute.

Rear Elbow Strikes

If we can manoeuvre our arms then we may be able to use our elbows to strike our attacker.

Depending on the type of grab, we can execute it high to the face or lower to the ribs of the opponent.

As it's a precursor technique, they don't have to be full power elbows, just strong enough to create the reaction we want, so simply throw your elbow straight backwards, instead of chambering it first.

In training, you should execute elbows to the face with extreme care, even using the back of your upper arm instead of the point of your elbow, for safety. For the mid section elbow, this can be done a little more vigorously, but still not full power.

Ripping

'Ripping' is a technique for removing yourself from a clothing grip and its so simple, most students do not even think of it! It is exactly what it says, ripping yourself from the grip, by simply pulling the affected limb away sharply.

In my classes, I talk about the 'Taekwon-Do grip'; something sadly lost to most instructors these days, but which appears as early as the pattern Won-Hyo. It first occurs on the 2nd movement, when you execute the knifehand inward strike. It is the returning fist that is actually the Taekwon-Do grip technique and its different from a standard grip, as it grabs onto the opponents clothing and twists it around the fist, making a release from it much more difficult.

However, the standard grip of an aggressor is usually much more basic and simply grabs the clothing without any twist of the fist at all and

The 'Taekwon-Do Grip' found in Won-Hyo tul

often, you can remove the grip by 'ripping' your arm away from it.

As soon as a clothing grab is applied, pull your arm backwards or away from the grip sharply to rip yourself out of the grip. This allows a potentially trapped limb, to be free for a counter strike, which often will surprise the opponent, making it much more likely that the strike will hit home!

In the following chapters, some of the defences show precursor techniques and some do not, it is really up to the student to decide when and if to use them to aid in their defences.

A Word About Headbutts

In most circumstances, headbutts are frowned upon as a form of self-defence, despite the fact they are often used offensively by aggressors! In my opinion however, they are a useful tool that should be, at the very least, understood and practiced by students, because if you don't practice them, you won't think to use them and if you don't understand them, then you are liable to injure yourself rather then the attacker!

Apart from being frowned upon, there is the train of thought that your head controls the rest of your body and thus you shouldn't risk damaging it, but, as headbutts are frowned upon, they become an unexpected technique to use against the aggressor, more so for women, as headbutts are considered very unladylike, making them an ideal surprise counter-attack.

They become really useful when used as part of your defence techniques against grabs, as for an opponent to grab you, especially in things like bear-hugs, you know they are close enough for the headbutt to be effective, as well as close enough that the aggressor won't be able to block them.

The main problems with students using headbutts is they telegraph them, this is secondary to most students thinking the only headbutt is the front headbutt; but there are side, rear and upward versions as well.

The general rule of the thumb with headbutts is the 'eyebrows'. This means, you should strike by using your head above your eyebrow line, to a place on the opponents head below their eyebrow line.

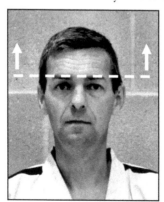 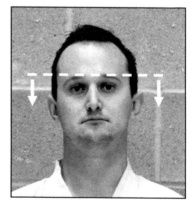

Defender on Attacker
When used as a self defence technique, the defender (left)
should try and use the area above the eyebrows to attack the
aggressor (right) to an area below the eyebrow level such as the
nose, cheek or mouth.

Types of Headbutts

Listed below are the various types of headbutt a student can employ for self-defence. Unlike the movies, a headbutt doesn't have to be a take out technique, but simply a precursor technique, that is used prior to other follow up techniques, due to the natural reaction it creates, which is often the attacker bringing his hands up to the area struck, thus loosening or releasing grips etc.

Front Headbutt

To execute suddenly and sharply thrust your head forwards, aiming for the attackers nose (which causes the eyes to water and often creates a lot of blood to aid in shocking the attacker), though anywhere on the lower part of the attackers face will hurt.

Rear Headbutt

To execute, suddenly and sharply thrust your head backwards. Do not move the head forwards before executing the backwards motion as this will alert the attacker to your intention commonly known as telegraphing. Again, aim for the nose, or even the mouth

Upward Headbutt

Can be used whether facing or turned around from your opponent and is ideal for taller opponents or one that may be pulling you downwards.

From a lower level than your opponents head, simply thrust straight upwards, sharply, aiming to hit under the jaw like a uppercut.

Side Headbutt

To execute, swing your head sideways sharply, aiming to hit the attacker on their cheekbone.

Training Headbutts

Headbutt practice in class is relatively straight forward. For speed and impact, as well as to practice non-telegraphing them, simply practice them on focus pads.

To understand where they should hit a human, practice them slowly, with a partner, with little (very light) to no contact.

If used in hosinsul practice, it is useful for the attacking student to understand what the usual (and natural) response to a headbutt would be and thus adjust his attack accordingly, such as loosening his grip if attacking with a front bear hug, as for safe training, students can obviously not go around headbutting each other.

Defences Against Lapel Grabs

A lapel grab (also termed collar grabs) can be executed single or double handed. They are often the precursor to a strike or a headbutt and thus need to be responded to quickly, with an eye towards defending the strike as well.

Single Lapel Grab - Defence 1
This is a very simple release, utilizing a low outer forearm block which is found in Saju Jirugi and Chon-Ji tul.

1a, 1b, 1c & 1d. As the attacker grabs your lapel, immediately chamber and execute a low outer forearm block, striking your attackers arm a couple of inches from his wrist (on the radial nerve) and using the rest of the block as follow through, as opposed to trying to stop it at the point of impact, as if you miss the pressure point, the follow through will still rip the attackers hand off, due to the fact the wrist can only bend a little when vertical.

Be sure to use the dropping into a walking stance to add force to your blocking arm. Also, if the attacker throws a punch quickly, the chamber position makes an ideal cover for your face.

2. Immediately follow up your release with a reverse punch or right cross punch.

Single Lapel Grab - Defence 2

For this defence, we use a slight variation of the first closed stance[10] ready postures the student comes across in the Ch'ang hon tul, namely moa junbi sogi 'A' and moa junbi sogi 'B'.

1a, 1b & 1c. As the attacker grabs your lapel, bring your right hand over and around your attackers wrist, then grip it and place your left hand on top and rotate the attackers arm 180 degrees so you are in the closed ready stance 'A' position.

Ideally, you want the arc of your hand around the wrist gap between the attackers forearm and hand.

2a & 2b. Keeping your grip on the opponents wrist, rotate your hands to the close ready stance 'A' position.

Note 1: The smaller the rotation of the wrist, means less effort will be required and it will be more

---

[10] Technically, the official term for the stance is 'close ready stance', but most use the terminology 'closed ready stance', so I have stayed with the most common term used by the majority.

effective.

Note 2: *If you find the wrist lock to be ineffective against a stronger opponent, move forwards and bend their elbow to a 90 degree angle, across the front of their body, then apply the lock.*

3. Follow up with a front snap kick to the opponents body or head, whilst maintaining your wrist lock.

Single Lapel Grab - Defence 3
For this defence, we use the palm upward block found in Joong-Gun tul.

1a, 1b & 1c. As the attacker grabs your lapel, immediately step inwards towards the attacker and execute the palm upward block from Joong-Gun tul.

2a & 2b. Keeping hold of the attackers arm, execute a side piercing kick to the front of the attackers knee joint.

3. If needed, follow up with a knifehand strike to the side of the attackers neck.

Single Lapel Grab - Defence 4

For this defence, we apply a basic wrist lock to the attacker.

1a, 1b & 1c. As the attacker grabs your lapel, execute a oblique kick to the opponents shin as a distraction (precursor technique). Grabbing their wrist as you do so.

Use your opposite hand for the initial grab, placing your own hand over the top of the opponents.

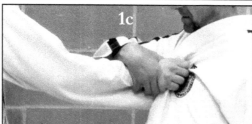

For practice, you can place your thumb directly on the back of your partners hand and wrap your fingers around the rest of it.

2a & 2b. Grab on with your other hand, so it is in the same position as your original grab, just on the opposite side and rotate their wrist clockwise in a small circle (so their fingers turn upwards - *see pic 3*), whilst stepping backwards.

3. Apply pressure to their wrist by pressing on the back of their hand with your thumbs, rotating their wrist, in a small circle towards them.

4. Finish with a front snap kick.

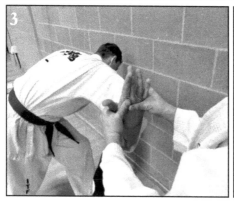

Double Lapel Grab - Defence 1

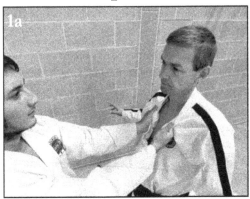

For this defence, we use the straight fingertip thrust that is found in Do-San tul.

1a & 1b. As the attacker grabs your lapels, bring your hands up. *In a real situation, it would be a good idea to keep your attacker engaged by talking to him, to disguise your hand movements.*

2. Trap the opponents arm by placing your left arm over both of theirs (the palm block part of the technique), whilst simultaneously thrusting your fingers into the opponents clavicle.

3 & 4. Step forwards into a walking stance to allow you to thrust further and harder until the attacker lets go. Follow up if needed.

Double Lapel Grab - Defence 2

For this defence, we use an angle punch first found in Joong-Gun tul, followed by a side elbow strike.

1a, 1b & 1c. As the attacker grabs your lapels, twist 90 degrees whilst executing an angle punch over the attackers arms, grabbing the attackers hands (with your left hand) and trapping them against your body.

2. Execute a side elbow strike directly to your opponents face.

3a, 3b & 3c. Extend your right arm to reach over the opponents shoulder, grabbing onto their clothing at the rear with your right hand, keeping your outer forearm along their face (cheek or jaw line), whilst still keeping a grip on their arms with your left hand. This is for control. *3c is the rear view of 3b.*

4. Follow up with knee strikes to the groin or body.

Double Lapel Grab - Defence 3

For this defence, we use the twin palm upward block found in Choong-Moo tul.

1a, 1b & 1c. As soon as your lapels are grabbed by the attacker, step backwards to straighten the attackers arms and execute the twin palm upward block to the attackers elbows.

Double Lapel Grab - Defence 4

For this defence, we use the palm upward block, combined with stepping into the angled sitting stance, found in Ge-Baek tul.

1a, 1b & 1c. As your lapels are grabbed by the attacker, step to the side at an angle to form a sitting stance and to avoid a possible headbutt, whilst at the same time placing your left palm on the side of the attackers elbow joint, executing the palm upward block in the circular motion (as in the pattern), pushing the attackers elbow upwards and inwards.

2. With the palm upward block executed, keep it pressed on the attackers elbow, keeping their arm/s trapped as you execute a punch with the opposite hand to the floating ribs.

1c & 2. Reversed view

3a, 3b & 3c. Following the punch (or simply not using it at all), you should be close enough to the attacker to release your palm and wrap your arm around their head, grabbing their jaw and twisting their head away from you, forcing them to bend backwards, leaving their throat exposed for a downward punch.

Alternatively, you could use the head grab to simply pull them off balance and straight down to the ground.

Defences Against Wrist Grabs

Wrist grabs can be executed single or doubled handed. Single wrist grabs can be executed as 'same side' grabs or 'cross-grabs'. Usually they are applied by grabbing on top of the defenders arms, but they can also come from underneath, so all varieties should be practiced.

Single 'same side' Wrist Grab - Defence 1

For this defence, we use the two palm hooking blocks we first encounter in Yul-Gok tul.

1a, 1b & 1c. As the attacker grabs your wrist, rotate your grabbed arm, so that your hand uses the palm hooking block motion, to travel around the inside of your opponents arm to finish on top of it.

2a & 2b. Quickly execute the second palm hooking block (with your opposite hand), to the side of the opponents head, striking it hard and bending their head side ways towards their shoulder. This block can also serve as a defence against a punch should they attack with their opposite hand.

3. Immediately follow up with a knee kick from your rear leg, to the attackers solar plexus or groin.

4. Finish with an elbow strike if required.

Single 'same side' Wrist Grab - Defence 2

Sometimes, the best defence is a good offence as the saying goes and this is precisely what we do, using the basic obverse forefist punch taught to all beginners in Taekwon-Do.

1a, 1b, 1c & 1d. As your wrist is grabbed by the attacker, simply step forwards and punch them in the face (the jaw being the best target).

To add extra impact to your strike, grab the attackers own arm (*pics 1b & 1c*) and pull it towards you as you strike.

Single 'same side' Wrist Grab - Defence 3

For this defence we turn a grabbed wrist into a wrist lock of our own, using the x-fist pressing block and pulling motion that 2nd degree's will recognise from pattern Choong-Jang tul.

1a, 1b & 1c. As your wrist is grabbed, immediately place your opposite arm underneath the attackers arm, in the x-fist pressing

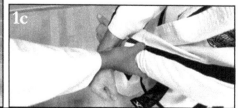

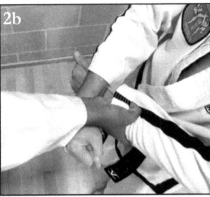

block position.

2a & 2b. As in the pattern, pull your 'block' up and backwards, whilst executing a knee kick at the same time.

Note: As you have trapped the attackers arm, it should turn palm upwards as you pull your block back, which locks the wrist *(see pic 2b)*.

Single 'same side' Wrist Grab - Defence 4

This is a basic wrist release that we teach all white belts at my Academy, as it utilizes a low outer forearm block that all 10th kups learn in Saju Jirugi.

1a, 1b & 1c. With your wrist grabbed, raise your opposite arm in preparation for the low outer forearm block release. It can also be used to defend against a punch (1c).

2a, 2b & 2c. Execute the low block, by striking the attackers arm about 2 inches

from their wrist, hitting it and following through to the standard blocking position.

3. Once released, follow up with strikes.

Single 'cross' Wrist Grab - Defence 1

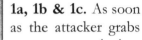

For this defence, we use a palm hooking block, found in Yul-Gok tul, followed by a low outer forearm block.

1a, 1b & 1c. As soon as the attacker grabs your wrist in a cross grab, rotate your wrist around the outside of the attackers arm, in the palm hooking block motion.

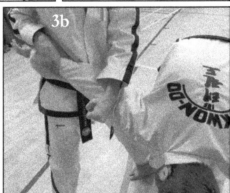

2. Grab onto the attackers arm.

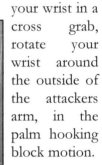

3a, 3b & 3c. Chamber and execute a low outer forearm block to the attackers tricep. Keeping the pressure on to apply an armlock.

4a & 4b. Finish up with a downward elbow strike to the attackers spine *(do not do this in training)*.

Single 'cross' Wrist Grab - Defence 2

Students who are 2nd kup and above will recognise the move we use for this defence, from Hwa-Rang tul, as it's the side elbow thrust. But they probably won't recognise the way we use it, not as a thrust, but as an armlock.

1a & 1b. As your wrist is grabbed by the opponent, spin around to the outside, placing your other arm over the top of the attackers (so its in your armpit) and grab hold of it with both hands.

2. Ensure you rotate their wrist so that the hand is 'thumb down', which means their elbow is up, then press down with your body weight, on the attackers elbow joint.

3. From here we have various options; we can break the attackers arm or simply hold them in the lock. If they struggle, we can quickly strike with the elbow as well.

Single 'cross' Wrist Grab - Defence 3

Once again we use the extremely useful palm hooking block (found in Yul-Gok tul) in our defence.

1a & 1b. As your wrist is grabbed by the opponent, rotate your palm around the outside of the attackers arm.

2a, 2b & 2c. As you 'hook' and grab onto your opponents arm, side step slightly and pull thier arm forwards, whilst at the same time executing a

reverse knifehand or forearm smash, to the back of their head.

3a & 3b. At this point, your grab and strike should see the attacker bent forwards and from here, you can execute a front rising kick as a final strike.

Single 'cross' Wrist Grab - Defence 4

For this defence, we use the high outer forearm side block first found in Do-San tul, to lock our attackers arm and avoid the attack.

1a & 1b. As your opponent grabs your wrist, raise your grabbed arm to the outside of the opponents arm and pivot 90 degrees (also to the outside of the opponent) - this helps to avoid the secondary blow by taking us away from the intended point of impact, as well as aiding us in locking the opponents arm.

locking the opponents arm.

Note: If we are too slow, we can still deflect the blow or take it on our arm.

2a, 2b & 2c. As we pivot, to avoid losing control of the opponents arm, place your other hand on the top of the opponents hand and sharply put the 'block' into place, which locks the opponents arm straight, as well as pulling their opposite shoulder in the opposite direction, nullifying their secondary attack (in this case a punch with the other hand).

3a & 3b. Following a successful defence/armlock, follow up with a counter-strike to the locked arm, using an elbow strike or in this case a backfist front strike (such as in Ge-Baek tul), as a forearm smash to the now straightened elbow joint.

Double Wrist Grab - Defence 1

For this defence, we are simply going to use the ready posture from Ul-Ji tul.

1a & 1b. As both your wrists are grabbed, bring your hands inwards and upwards, crossing them as you do so.

1c. Either your wrists will be released or the attacker will have a weakened grip on you.

2a & 2b. With the grip released or loosened, follow up by executing a front snap kick to the attackers groin. Alternatively use a front rising kick if you are too close.

Double Wrist Grab - Defence 2

For this defence, we are going to use a simple low outer forearm block to release both hands.

1a & 1b. As both your wrists are grabbed begin to chamber for the low outer forearm block by twisting your right arm anti-clockwise whilst moving it towards (and above) your left arm. Do this sharply and the twist will cause it to release through the gap between the attackers finger and thumb.

2a & 2b. From the chamber position, execute the low outer forearm block, striking it down hard onto your opponents forearm, aiming to hit the radial nerve, which is about 2 inches from the opponents wrist.

3. Immediately follow up with striking techniques.

Double Wrist Grab - Defence 3

For this defence, we use a couple of techniques that are both found in Joong-Gun tul, namely the twin upset punch to x-fist rising block.

1a, 1b, 1c & 1d. As both your wrists are grabbed bring your hands to the inside of the attackers, rotating them around and onto the attackers forearms, gripping onto them. Once gripped, continue rotating into the twin upset punch position.

2a & 2b. With your grip in place, raise the attackers arms and execute a spot-turn to bring your shoulder underneath the

attackers elbow joints - the x-fist rising block portion of the defence - at this point one or both of the attackers elbow joints will be pointing down and one of their arms should be locked straight.

3. From your current position, you can forcefully pull the attackers arms down onto your shoulder to break or damage their elbow joint or...

4a, 4b & 4c. ... you can execute a very painful throw by dropping your weight (as you place the attackers locked arm/s over your shoulder), then straightening up and bending forwards to execute the throw.

Double Wrist Grab - Defence 4
This is a very simple defence using the side pressing kick, found in Kwang-Gae tul.

1a, 1b, 1c & 1d. As your wrists are seized, turn your body side on (step back or forward if necessary) and execute a side pressing kick, sharply to the inside of the attackers knee joint.

As it's a pressing kick, do not retract the kick but press it down towards the ground.

Notes: If pushed or pulled via this grab, turning side on will allow you to drop into a sitting stance if needed, for stability. Also, pulling your arms back from the attacker, will distract from your true intention of counter-attacking with your leg.

Double Rear Wrist Grab - Defence 1

For this defence, we use a back snap kick, followed by a back piercing kick.

1a, 1b & 1c. As both your wrists or arms are grabbed from behind, immediately execute a back snap kick to the attackers groin.

As the attacker will most likely be directly behind you, there is no need to look back first, just use your own body as a guide of where to kick and the attackers inner thighs will do the rest if you are slightly off target.

2a & 2b. As the attacker recoils from the kick (likely bending over whilst moving his groin away from the pain), use the distance to execute a back piercing kick.

Double Rear Wrist Grab - Defence 2

For this defence, we use a twin fist middle front punch, which unfortunately is first found in Tong-Il tul, yet is an easy way for all students to effect a release from a double rear wrist grab.

1a, 1b, 1c & 1d. As the attacker grabs both your wrists from behind, immediately bend your elbows and execute a twin fist middle front punch, while stepping forwards into a walking stance.

2. Once released, immediately execute a side elbow thrust as a counter attack.

Double Rear Wrist Grab - Defence 3

This defence is for an attacker, who has grabbed both your wrists from behind and is quite close to you.

1a & 1b. As the attacker grabs both your wrists from behind, immediately execute a rear headbutt by simply throwing your head backwards sharply - do not telegraph your intentions by bringing your head forwards first!

Ideally, we hope to hit the nose (for the pain it causes), but anywhere on the attackers face will do…

2a & 2b. … as the natural reaction to being headbutted in the face is to bring your hands up to the affected area, thus releasing the grip and as they do so, spin round and execute a knifehand side strike to the attackers neck (carotid artery).

Two Handed Single Wrist Grab - Defence 1

To obtain a release from a grab with both arms, we are going to use a familiar technique from Hwa-Rang tul; the downward knifehand strike, to release our arm and counter-attack in the same motion.

1a & 1b. With both the opponents hands clamped around your (single) arm, start rotating your arm towards you, bending your elbow as you do so.

2. Keep rotating your arm in a circular motion and the opponent will find it really difficult to hold on and will loosen their grip on you.

3a & 3b. Simply continue the circular motion, bringing your hand downwards again and execute the knifehand downward strike, before following up.

Two Handed Single Wrist Grab - Defence 2

Another way to obtain a release from a grab with both arms is to bring your grabbed arm straight through the middle of the attackers grab.

1a & 1b. As your arm is grabbed by both hands of the attacker, pull your arm straight up through the centre. If you find that the opponent can resist your release, place your other hand on the top of your closed fist for extra leverage *(see pictures below)*.

2a & 2b. If the range is right, you can continue the release motion and turn it into an upper elbow strike to the jaw or solar plexus.

Two handed Version

If you struggle with executing the previous release with one hand, simply grab the hand you need to release with your other hand and pull upwards sharply.

Two Handed Single Wrist Grab - Defence 3

Most students that are 2nd Kup or above will know this release technique, as its found 'as is' in Hwa-Rang tul, though this version has some slight variations.

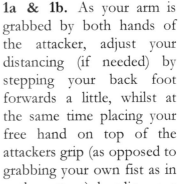

1a & 1b. As your arm is grabbed by both hands of the attacker, adjust your distancing (if needed) by stepping your back foot forwards a little, whilst at the same time placing your free hand on top of the attackers grip (as opposed to grabbing your own fist as in the pattern), bending your elbow towards you as you do so.

Grabbing the attackers grip is so they don't release their grip and nullify our technique.

2a , 2b & 2c. Execute a side piercing kick, but to the attackers upper thigh (which will lock their leg) and, as you make contact with your kick, pull your arm free.

Note: In Hwa-Rang tul, the height of the kick is mid section, but as you can see from the picture below, it can leave the attackers hands very close to the kickers leg, which means they may be able to grab it, even if you do secure a release.

Two Handed Single Wrist Grab - Defence 4

The defence for this attack takes into account the fact that the attacker is using both his hands, whilst the defender still has a hand free.

1a, 1b & 1c. As the attacker grabs your arms, pull it backwards so it looks like your focus is on releasing it, but instead, as you draw the attacker forwards strike the side of his face with a 'power slap' using your free hand.

2a & 2b. A power slap is more like a palm strike than an actual slap (which is often executed with the fingers), as it uses the more solid palm of the hand to strike.

However, where it differs from a standard palm strike is there is no telegraphing the technique i.e. you do not draw your arm back to gain power. You (speedily) bring your arm straight up and sharply twist your hips as you strike the target, which in this case is the jaw (2a) or as an alternative, you can cup your hand slightly and strike the attackers ear (2b).

Defences Against Armlocks

Whilst some Taekwon-Do schools teach armlocks and how to put them on, very few teach how to escape from them and when it comes to armlocks, which press down on the elbow joints or lock up the shoulder joint, they become very painful, very quickly and so, the first step in their defence is to remove the leverage the opponent has gained, thus removing both the pain and the threat of a broken arm (if an armbar), allowing us to counter-attack properly.

Standing Armbar/Armlock - Defence 1
This defence simply uses the understanding of how the elbow joint works and uses this knowledge to release the pressure, prior to counter attacking.

1a, 1b & 1c. As the armbar/armlock is applied and pressure is increased by the attacker, rotate your trapped arm towards the attacker, so the elbow turns from an upward position, to a downward position, leaving the armbar/armlock ineffective.

2a & 2b. Whilst the attackers arms are still engaged, counter attack with your free arm, using a punch, or in this case, an arc-hand strike.

Standing Armbar/Armlock - Defence 2

Again, this defence uses the understanding of how the elbow joint works to release the pressure, but in doing so leaves the attacker exposed for an initial elbow thrust.

1a, 1b & 1c. As the attacker applies his armbar/armlock, pivot round and turn into it, bending your elbow as you do so. This takes away the pressure of the armbar/armlock and even though your opponent will still have a grip on your arm, your elbow is now pointing directly towards the opponents chest.

2. Immediately thrust the point of your elbow sharply into the attackers chest.

3. Follow up with other counter-strikes.

Standing Armbar/Armlock - Defence 3

This defences turns the attackers armbar/armlock and converts it into an armbar/armlock on them!

1a & 1b. As the armbar/armlock is applied on you, immediately step your closest foot (to the attacker) forwards while reaching for and grabbing the attackers wrist or arm.

2. Grabbing onto the attackers arm, sharply pull it across your body.

3. You now have the attackers arm locked in front of you and with the stepping forwards of your foot, you now are in a good position for the best leverage, so push your shoulder forwards, turning slightly and dropping your weight, to apply the armbar/armlock fully onto the attacker..

Half-Nelson - Defence 1

Half-Nelson's are extremely painful, so action needs to be taken quickly. For defences/escapes from half-nelson grabs we find the answers in Do-San tul, specifically the release technique, although its not used in the prescribed way, as it is actually the part after the straight fingertip thrust release (when we spin) that we use to escape this grip.

1a & 1b. As your arm is grabbed and pulled up behind your back, completely forget about the grabbed arm, relaxing all the muscles in your shoulder and spin around 90 degrees.

2 (a, b or c). Using the motion of the spin, strike the attackers head (preferably the side of their jaw), with your free hand/arm. As you strike, its likely the attacker will release their grip, but just in case, pull your arm out of their grip at the moment you strike.

2a, 2b & 2c. What's good about using the spin and backfist strike from Do-San tul, is that it covers a range of distances.

It is likely that your attacker will be very close, hence you can strike with your chambered backfist i.e. your elbow. (2a).

If they are too far away for a spinning elbow strike, you can strike with your forearm, to their neck (carotid artery). (2b)

Finally, if they are fairly far away (which is unlikely), you can strike with the actual backfist strike itself, to their temple or jaw. (2c)

2b. Striking with the forearm

Half-Nelson - Defence 2

This is a variation of the last defence and again uses the same techniques found in Do-San tul, but ends up with a throw to the opponent. In this attack, we have also included a rear collar grab, as it often accompanies a half-nelson.

1a, 1b. & 1c. As your arm is grabbed and pulled up behind your back, rotate 90 degrees away from the opponent (on the side of the grabbed arm) into a sitting stance, gripping onto the opponents arm (with your grabbed arm) and as you do so, execute the backfist strike, with your free arm, to their floating ribs.

2a, 2b & 2c. Immediately following the backfist strike, bring your striking arm, over the attackers arm and wrap it around both their arms. If they haven't already released their half-nelson (due to the backfist) or even if they have, apply pressure to the attackers elbow joint by pressing your wrapped arm inwards against it.

3. With both the attackers arms locked with your own, continue the spin and wrap your (now) free arm around their back

4. As you wrap your arm around the opponents back, position your feet for a hip throw by stepping them parallel , whilst at the same time lowering your centre of gravity and bucking your hips backwards into the opponent to break their balance.

5a, 5b, 5c, 5d & 5e. Straighten your legs and execute a hip throw, throwing the opponent to the ground in front of you.

6a, 6b, 6c & 6d. Alternatively, depending on how good your throwing skills are, you can execute a shoulder throw instead of a hip throw, by bringing your free arm under the attackers instead.

Full Nelsons

Full Nelson's are very dangerous if applied properly. Unlike the movie or American Wrestling versions, which are for show, a proper **full nelson** exerts a lot of pressure on your upper spine and can quickly lead to a compression

fracture in your neck or upper back (*see left picture*), so action needs to be taken immediately.

As the head is pressed downwards, one way to help relieve the pressure is via the use of 'heaven hand', by bringing both the back of your hands to your forehead and using them to help resist the downwards pressure of the attacker (*see right picture*). This counter-defence will often be the first thing you need to do, prior to the actual escape.

Full Nelson - Defence 1

For this first defence, we will use the knifehand strike to **palm that we find in Kwang-Gae tul.**

1a, 1b & 1c. Whilst the full nelson hold is on, explosively execute the knifehand to palm technique, just as you do in Kwang-Gae tul, sharply bringing one hand to the other, which will break the opponents hold.

2. Momentarily trap the opponents arms under your armpits, by grabbing one of your arms and squeezing them both inwards, which makes it hard for the attacker to escape.

3a & 3b. Grab the opponents arm, so it can't be used in defence, then immediately execute a rear elbow strike to the attackers head - keep striking!

Full Nelson - Defence 2

For this defence, we are going to exploit the weak point in any grip, the finger joints!

1a & 1b. With the full nelson hold applied, drop your weight down, to allow you to reach over your head and grab onto the opponents hands. It will also help alleviate some of the pressure.

2a & 2b. Take hold of one or more of the opponents fingers, rip it away and their hand will follow, releasing their grip.

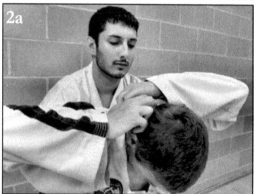 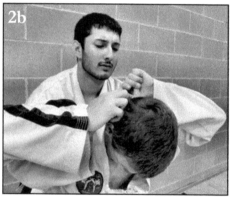

3a & 3b. Keeping hold of the opponents fingers, bring them down to your side.

4a & 4b. Side step slightly and strike a side fist into their groin, then strike straight upwards with an elbow strike.

Full Nelson - Defence 3

This defence uses a reverse hip throw to take down the attacker and escape.

1a & 1b. Take some of pressure off your neck by bringing your hands up to your forehead.

2a & 2b. Step one leg backwards, between you and the attacker, so your hip is behind the attackers hip.

3a & 3b. Reach down and wrap your arms around the attackers legs.

4a, 4b & 4c. Straighten up whilst still grasping the attackers legs, so that they fall backwards over your hip and dump them head first onto the ground.

Full Nelson - Defence 4

This defence uses the combination of techniques that we find at the beginning of Ul-Ji tul.

Note: The photographs for this defence run from right to left, as the student and attacker are moving backwards (the same as in pattern Ul-Ji)

1a, 1b & 1c. As the full nelson hold is applied, secure your head/neck from further pressure, by placing both hands on your forehead and immediately start stepping backwards - step to the outside of the opponent, so one of their legs is between yours. Press your hips back into them as you step back.

2a & 2b. Continue backwards, by stepping your other leg back, leaning down and grabbing the opponents leg (at the calf) with both your hands. By now, your opponents leg should be locked straight, between your legs!

3a, 3b & 3c. Continue pressing back with your hips and pull upwards on the opponents leg, ensuring you don't pull it straight into your own groin (pull it slightly to the side to avoid that). With the opponent already off-balanced from you stepping back into them, the pulling of the leg should be enough to topple them over and from there, you can turn and execute a low side kick to them or even turn them and apply a leg lock as seen on page 154.

Defences Against Bear Hugs

A bear hug is any grab where the opponent wraps their arms around your upper body. The most common of which is from behind and over both arms, but they can also be performed from behind and under the arms, as well as from the front and side. The final fact you need to include is that the placement can be high on the upper arms or low, around the forearms. Practicing against an attempted bear hug (one that doesn't quite get a strong secure wrap, due to fast reflexes of the defender) is also recommended.

Attempted Rear Bear Hug - Defence 1
3rd degrees and above will recognise this defence as the first few moves from Yoo-Sin tul.

1a, 1b & 1c. As you feel the opponents arms wrapping around your own, quickly drop your weight by stepping your left foot out, whilst raising both arms to a horizontal position.

2a & 2b. Hook one arm under the opponents and grab their upper sleeve with your other hand.

3a & 3b. Buck your hips backwards, into the opponent and lean forwards, pulling the opponents arm and execute a shoulder throw.

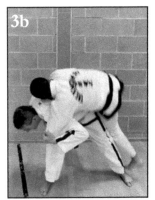

4. With the opponent on the floor in front of you, follow up by breaking their elbow joint with your knee or foot strikes (stamps).

Attempted Rear Bear Hug - Defence 2
This is a simple, yet effective way to avoid a bear hug attack.

1a, 1b & 1c. As the opponent attempts to bear hug you, immediately throw your arms upwards, whilst dropping down onto one knee.

2. Execute a rear elbow thrust to the opponents groin.

Note: Both of the previous attempted rear bear hug defences can also work against a full bear hug (that has gripped you), though if used that way, then a precursor technique, such as a rear headbutt or foot stamp is a good idea before executing the release.

Rear Bear Hug - Defence 1

For this escape, we will use a combination that 4th degree's may recognise from Ul-Ji tul.

1a & 1b. To start with, we take the focus away from the attackers grab by executing a rear headbutt. In practice, do this lightly and ensure the opponents head is facing away. Alternatively you can execute any other precursor technique.

2a & 2b. With the opponent temporarily stunned, we step backwards, ensuring we step to the outside of the opponents leg. We use our hands to help create extra

room in-between the attackers arm by grabbing them and pulling them outwards as we step back (the 1st move of Ul-Ji).

Note: *As in the actual pattern, if needed, should the attacker move back as well, step back twice.*

3a & 3b. Having broken the attackers balance, we find that the attackers leg is between our own and we have some room to move, so reach down and grab the attackers leg with both hands.

4. Pull the attackers leg upwards as you sit on it, which will cause the attacker to fall backwards as we apply pressure (via our body weight and gravity) to the locked leg of our opponent.

5a, 5b & 5c. With the attacker down, slip your hands up to their foot and twist it (via the toes) in the direction you want them to roll over, so as to move them onto their front.

6a, 6b & 6c. From this position we have the option to run, finish with strikes (foot stamps or kicks) or perform a leg lock! As we turn the opponent, we follow the leg and step with it (in this case with our right foot), so that that our foot is now between the attackers legs, with their leg pressed against our inner thigh.

7a & 7b. From this position we simply lean forwards to lock the leg and increase the pain. The more we lean into it, the more it hurts! If you move your other leg forwards, you can maintain your balance as well as the lock, enabling you to strike or grab the attackers head.

Rear Bear Hug - Defence 2
This release technique works due to a natural instinct.

1a, 1b, 1c, 1d, 1e, 1f & 1g. Instead of executing a single strike to the attackers groin with a closed fist (that may miss), instead use an open hand slap to the groin. To do this, move your hips from side to side to expose the attackers groin and slap backwards to it, alternating your hands on each slap. Keep going until you feel the attacker slacken their bear hug.

2. The natural instinct of the attacker is to protect their groin, which makes them move their hips backwards, creating space for you to execute a side or rear elbow thrust to their solar plexus.

3. The previous elbow would likely have made the attacker bend forwards, so follow up with an upward elbow strike to the attackers jaw.

Rear Bear Hug - Defence 3

For this defence, we are using a variation of the twin side elbow thrust that we find in Yul-Gok tul.

1a & 1b. Form your hands into fists and use the knuckle of your finger joints *(see pic 2b)* to strike into the small bones on the back of the attackers hands, on their grip. Strike hard!

2a & 2b. Keep striking the same way, but alternate you fists.

3. Keep striking until the opponent releases their grip, then follow up with a rear elbow thrust and other strikes as needed.

Rear Bear Hug - Defence 4

This is a rear bear hug escape that utilises the motion of a low outer forearm block, that all students of Taekwon-Do learn when they first start training.

1a & 1b. As the attackers grip goes on, try to raise your arms into the chamber position, which will give you some room to manoeuvre.

2. At the same time you raise your arms, slip one foot back and then behind the opponents legs (in a walking stance position).

3a, 3b & 3c. As you execute the low block, optionally strike the opponent with your elbow, then continue to execute the low block in its entirety, which will force the opponent backwards, tripping over your leg.

4a & 4b. Finish up with a foot stamp to the opponents chest.

Rear Bear Hug (under arms) - Defence 1
The finger joints are a weak area of the human body, so we use that knowledge to create a release.

1a & 1b. As you feel the attack around your waist, quickly stamp on the attackers foot as a distraction technique.

2a & 2b. As the pain of the foot stamp distracts the opponent, try to grab one of their fingers and violently bend it backwards.

3. Keep hold of the finger as you pull it far enough to fully release the grip.

4. Execute a rear elbow thrust to the opponents face.

Rear Bear Hug (under arms) - Defence 2

This release uses your head and elbows to escape from the attackers bear hug.

1a & 1b. As the attacker grabs around your waist, throw your head backwards and execute a rear headbutt.

2a & 2b. The attacker will move their head backwards following the headbutt, giving you better distance to follow up by using rear elbow strikes.

3a & 3b. If the first strike doesn't force the attacker to release their grip, they will instead,

move their head away from the point of impact, so continue executing elbow strikes, alternating your arms.

4a & 4b. Continue with elbow strikes, as needed, until you feel the attacker release their grip from around your waist. They will also likely back away.

5a & 5b. As soon as you feel the release, turn and follow up with more strikes while the attacker is dazed from your previous elbow strikes.

Rear Bear Hug (under arms) - Defence 3

This defence turns things around on the attacker, leaving them in a choke of our own.

1a & 1b. As the attacker grabs around your waist, immediately elbow them in the side of the head, which should give you a bit of 'wiggle' room or release their grip altogether.

2. Follow the momentum of the elbow strike, turning around as you do so, whilst extending your arm out and around the attackers neck.

3a & 3b. Continue looping your arm right around the attackers neck until your

forearm is underneath their throat and then immediately straighten your legs and pull up tightly with your arm to create a guillotine choke.

4. (*shown in reversed view*). From this position, you can continue with the choke and also attack with a knee strike as well.

Reversed view of applying the guillotine choke (after the elbow strike) with the knee strike follow up

Rear Bear Hug (under arms) - *Lifted* - Defence 4
The first part of this defence is getting the attacker to let go and to do this, you'll use back snap kicks and rear elbow strikes.

1a, 1b & 1c. As you are lifted off the floor by the attacker, immediately start kicking your legs backwards, performing back snap kicks, attempting to kick the opponent in the groin - this may cause them to let go of you straight away.

Ensure you kick quite a few times, whilst struggling in the grip as well.

2a, 2b & 2c. Switch from low level attacks to high level attacks and start continuously striking backwards with your elbow to the attackers head repeatedly.

3a & 3b. With the attackers bear hug released, either add another elbow strike whilst they are close or turn and continue with follow up techniques.

Front Bear Hug (over arms) - Defence 1
Sometimes, when your limbs are trapped, you should use **your head!**

1a, 1b, 1c & 1d. With your arms trapped against your sides by the attacker, draw your head back a little (not too much so you telegraph your intentions), and headbutt your attacker in the face. *Note:* The general rules for making a front headbutt effective is to use your head above the eyebrow line, whilst attacking the aggressor with it below thier eyebrow line (1d).

2a & 2b. As soon as the attacker releases you, follow up with a knee kick.

Front Bear Hug (over arms) - Defence 2

For this defence we use a rear foot stance to break the opponents balance.

1a & 1b. As soon as the attacker wraps their arms around you, place one foot behind the attackers leg.

2. Withdraw your front foot

to form a rear foot stance, which should hit the opponents knee joint and bend it, whilst at the same time grabbing the opponents waist with your hands and leaning your whole body forwards. If the opponent releases their grab, either continue and take them down or start striking.

Be warned that it is easy to fall with the opponent if they hold on, but on the plus side, you will land, with your whole body weight on top of the opponent, most likely knocking the wind out of them, allowing you a gap to follow up from the ground.

Front Bear Hug (over arms) - Defence 3
This defence uses an upward knee kick, first seen in Choong-Moo tul, but without the head grab.

1a & 1b. As the attacker bear hugs you, immediately execute an upward knee kick to their groin. There is no need to look, as the attacker is a mirror image of you (in positioning), so your centre, is their centre, plus if you are slightly off target, their own thighs will help guide the kick to its target.

2a & 2b. If you struck hard enough, the attacker will have released their grip, as it's a natural instinct to cover the groin after being hit, so take the opportunity to follow up with a knifehand inward strike to their

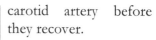

carotid artery before they recover.

Front Bear Hug (over arms) - Defence 4

This defence is for the more advanced student. It requires good balance and uses the reverse hooking kick that 2nd degree's performed in slow motion when performing Juche tul, however, in this case, it is executed at full speed.

1a, 1b & 1c. With the bear hug in place, slip your leg between the attackers legs and turn it into the side piercing kick position by locking your leg out sideways, whilst grabbing hold of the attacker.

Pictures below: The same sequences, but from a different angle for clarity

2a, 2b, 2c & 2d. Immediately start executing the reverse hooking kick, pivoting around sharply, whilst hooking the attackers leg on top of yours, by bending at the knee.

Use your hands to help turn the opponent in the same direction, pushing them to lose their balance (2b).

As you feel them losing balance and loosening their grip, hook your leg up as high as possible, whilst throwing them backwards with your hands (2c & 2d).

Note: It is easy to lose balance yourself, with this technique, so if you do, try to fall directly on top of your opponent, landing as heavily on them as possible, just not in training.

Side Bear Hug (over arms) - Defence 1

Whilst side bear hugs may not be as common as front or rear bear hug attacks, they do occur and its good to know some form of defence against them. Once the defence is initiated, a multitude of follow ups can be employed, simply by turning to face the opponent. In this instance we use a side headbutt to start the release process.

1a & 1b. As the attacker wraps their arms around you, violently (without telegraphing) thrust your head sideways and execute a side headbutt, loosening or releasing their hold.

2. Immediately follow your side headbutt by turning towards your opponents and grabbing thir testicles (if male) or inside thigh (and twist) - *In training just grab the inside of your partners leg.*

3. Instinctively, the opponent will likely grab your grabbing arm, so immediately follow up with a right cross to their jaw, releasing your arm as you do so.

Front Bear Hug (under arms) - Defence 1

If an attacker grabs you in a bear hug, but leaves your arms free, then you

have both hands to cause them immense pain!

1a, 1b & 1c. With the attackers arms tied up around your waist, immediately cup both your hands and strike both the opponents ears at the same time.

1c - *Close up*

Whilst hitting the ears with palms will hurt, cupping your hands (2) ensures air is driven into the opponents ears which may cause their ear drums to burst - so don't do this in training, as its dangerous and very painful!

Front Bear Hug (under arms) - Defence 2

For this defence we use a variation of twin vertical punch, that we first come across in Joong-Gun tul, except we don't use it as a punch to the jaw (like the standard application taught), but as a double eye gouge!

1a & 1b. As the attacker grabs you, bring your arms up and grab their head around their temples. (This can help defend against a headbutt, if that was the attackers intention).

2 - *Close up*

2. As your fingers make contact with their head, press your thumbs into the attackers eye sockets and thrust your arms forward quickly.

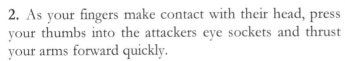

Front Bear Hug (under arms) - *Lifted* - Defence 3

If we are lifted up in a bear hug, it means both the attackers arms are engaged whilst both our arms are free, so for this defence we use the twin knifehand inward strike, found in both Juche and Ko-Dang tul.

1a & 1b. As you are lifted off the floor, in the bear hug, use both hands and execute the twin knifehand inward strike to each side of the attackers neck (the carotid arteries).

2. Keep striking until the attacker drops you and immediately counter attack.

Defences Against Hair Grabs

Although in itself, a hair grab is not too dangerous an attack, it can often be quite debilitating to the defender, because of the shock of it. More so, as the hair is attached to the head, it is a form of head control that can lead to much worse.

As pain thresholds vary from student to student, my first advice would be to simply get used to the pain caused, as that will allow you not to be shocked by it and respond properly.

Front Hair Grab - Defence 1
This defence is very simple and uses either a front rising kick, that many students learn at 10th kup or the front snap kick we first see in Do-San tul.

1a & 1b. As your hair is grabbed, help alleviate the pain by placing both hands on top of the attackers hand, pressing down as you do so. This will also help should you have to resist being pulled by the opponent, as you can use both your arms to resist.

2a & 2b. With a secure grip on one of your opponents hands, execute a low front snap kick or front rising kick to your attackers groin, which will be hard to block with one hand or for the attacker to dip down to block, as you have their other hand secured up high.

Front Hair Grab - Defence 2
This defence disrupts the attackers balance, whilst at the same time using his natural instincts against him.

front hair grab defences if needed.

2. Many Taekwon-Do students are geared to kick above the waist, due to sparring and dojang rules. But a back piercing kick to the thigh of the attacker is a great alternative as it can cause damage to the attackers leg/knee, meaning in a real life situation, it would be hard for the attacker to give chase, following a successful defence.

However, care must be taken when practicing this in the dojang.

Front or Rear Hair Grab - Defence 2

This defence can be used whether the students hair is grabbed from the front or rear and turns the attack into an armlock.

1a & 1b. As your hair is grabbed immediately trap the opponents hands on your head by placing both your hands on top of them. If pulled from the rear, spin around whilst maintaining the grip on the aggressors hands.

2a Step in, releasing one hand of the grip and place your forearm on the attackers tricep, whilst keeping your other hand on the attackers.

2b & 2c. Rotate your arm (to rotate the attackers arm) and press down on the attackers arm to lock it.

Rear Hair Grab - Defence 3

This is a defence that comes directly from Dan-Gun tul. I actually know of someone who was harassed as she walked past a group of teenagers, she tried to ignore them and keep on walking, but they grabbed her ponytail and pulled her backwards, she fell to the floor and they attacked her, hence it's a good defence to know if you have long hair!

1a & 1b. As the attacker grabs your hair and starts pulling you backwards, use the momentum and go with the pull…

2a, 2b & 2c. … but as you do so, pivot and turn into an L-stance or sitting stance (to regain balance) whilst at the same time, executing a knifehand side strike to the attackers neck or jaw.

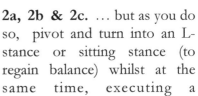

Defences Against Shoulder Grabs

Like most grabs, a shoulder grab is often a precursor to a strike, but can also be applied simply to pull you somewhere or pull you off-balance. Most shoulder grabs with a single grip occur on the same side, but, like double shoulder grabs, can be used from the front and the rear.

Single Shoulder Grab - Defence 1
For this shoulder grab defence we use the side pressing kick we first come across in Kwang-Gae tul. We can also use the following moves in the pattern as well, but as we are hoping to damage or break the attackers knee, they are unlikely to be necessary.

1a, 1b & 1c. As your shoulder is grabbed by the attacker, turn side on whilst grabbing the attackers own arm. If they attempt to pull you, turning side on will help you resist being pulled over, as you can drop into a sitting stance if need be.

2a & 2b. As soon as possible, raise your closest leg and execute a side pressing kick to the opponents knee joint, maintaining the grip on their arm for balance. Kick sharply at the joint.

3. As you are executing a side pressing kick, not a side piercing kick, ensure you keep 'pressing' into the attackers joint with your foot sword, which will either break or damage

their knee or at the very least, force them to turn away, so they can bend their knee to alleviate the pain of the attack, allowing you to follow up with strikes or even a choke (depending on their distance from you).

Single Shoulder Grab - Defence 2

For this defence we use the palm upward block that we first come across in Joong-Gun tul.

1a, 1b & 1c. As your shoulder is grabbed immediately twist your shoulders, placing one hand on top of the attackers grab to secure it. The shoulder twist will help ensure you lock their arm straight. Execute a palm upward block to the attackers elbow joint, ensuring their arm is locked straight when you do so, so that you damage or break their arm.

2a & 2b. While the attacker is distracted with the pain, step your front foot behind theirs and either sweep them or trip them over. Place your front hand to their shoulder, and push them as you trip or sweep them.

3. Once the attacker is down,

either run (if it's a real situation) or follow up by dropping sharply onto their body with your knee, then striking them.

Single Shoulder Grab - Defence 3
For this defence we use a reverse back fist strike.

1a, 1b & 1c. As your shoulder is grabbed use one hand to trap the attackers grab to your shoulder, whilst chambering (then striking) with your other hand.

The chamber position can also serve as a defensive block if needed, by covering your head and face.

2a, 2b or 2c. Strike with a back fist, forearm or knifehand, depending on the distance of the attacker and/or your preferred strike, keeping hold of the attackers arm.

3a & 3b. Take advantage of the attackers 'shock' from the strike, grab onto your opposite hand and bring your elbow over the attackers elbow, using your grip to rotate the arm, so their elbow is upwards.

4. Once your arm is over the attackers, press down sharply with your upper arm on either the attackers elbow joint or the attackers upper arm, forming an arm lock.

Single Shoulder Grab from the rear - Defence 1
For this defence we use a back fist strike followed by a basic wrist lock.

1a, 1b & 1c. As your shoulder is grabbed spin around (to the side of the grab) and execute a back fist strike to the attackers floating ribs, whilst grabbing and trapping their grabbing hand with your own.

2a & 2b. Whilst the attacker

is stunned from the back fist strike, quickly use both your hands to apply a basic wrist lock, by rotating their hand outwards.

Double Front Shoulder Grab - Defence 1

In this instance, we react to this grab by utilising the head grab and upward knee kick found in Choong-Moo tul.

1a & 1b. As soon as your shoulders are grabbed, bring your hands up and secure the attackers arms by pressing down on their arms. This helps with your own balance and will stop the attacker moving too far backwards, so the impact of the knee kick is stronger.

2. Simultaneously, as you grab, strike the attackers groin with your upward knee kick.

Double Front Shoulder Grab - Defence 2

This defence basically uses an angle punch (and the 90 degree turn) as found in Joong-Gun tul, with follow ups.

1a, 1b & 1c. As the attacker grabs your shoulders, raise one arm higher than the grab and sharply pivot 90 degrees, trapping both the attackers arms, under your own.

2. Use your other hand to secure the attackers arms, whilst you strike them with a side elbow thrust.

3a, 3b, 3c & 3d. Immediately follow on from the side elbow thrust by extending your arm and wrapping around the back of the opponents neck and underneath their throat and execute a guillotine choke, by straightening your legs and pulling upwards while your arm is tight across their larynx.

4. Whilst holding them in the choke, follow up with knee kicks.

Double Rear Shoulder Grab - Defence 1

For this defence we use a back snap kick, followed by a **side pressing kick**, as found in Kwang-Gae tul.

1a & 1b. As soon as you feel the attackers hands are on your shoulders, flick your leg backwards and upwards, executing a back snap kick to the opponents groin.

There is no need to even look, as their

centre will roughly be in the same place as yours.. Just behind! Do not chamber either, just flick the kick straight upwards behind you.

2a & 2b. Whilst the opponent is distracted by your first kick, quickly rechamber and sharply execute a side pressing kick to their upper thigh, just above their knee, pressing down in an attempt to damage their knee joint.

Unwanted Arm Around Shoulder - Defence 1

This is an ideal defence for someone who is receiving unwanted attention, perhaps from someone who is drunk and being over familiar! It uses the 'W' block from Toi-Gye tul to take the attacker down.

1a & 1b. With the unwanted arm around your shoulder, raise up your arm (one half of the 'W' block), behind your opponents arm.

2. Pull away slightly from the opponent if you need to create space and strike your forearm into the back of the opponents arm, just above the elbow joint, not on it and not to close to the opponents shoulder joint either.

3. With the lock in place, spin around whilst at the same time lowering your body to take the opponent to the ground.

Unwanted Arm Around Shoulder - Defence 2

This defence is fairly simple and uses the middle turning punch that we find in Eui-Am tul.

1a, 1b & 1c. With the unwanted arm dangled around your shoulder, turn 90 degrees into the aggressor and strike them in the solar plexus with the turning punch.

2a & 2b. As the aggressor reacts to the punch, quickly step backwards, wrapping your other arm over the attackers and pull down sharply, just before the elbow joint.

Chapter 6
Defences Against Chokes & Strangles

Cupping Technique

'Cupping' is a way of releasing the pressure of a choke or strangle, giving you some 'breathing room' (literally), allowing you to fight back sooner instead of fighting against the choke or strangle itself, as it starves you of oxygen. It may also give you some room to manoeuvre.

Cupping works like this: Instead of grabbing onto the arm that is choking you (which would be a usual response), form your hands into 'cups', with your thumb out of the way (see picture). Forcefully

bring both hands down together on the choking arm, dropping your body weight slightly, which should (if done sharply enough) cause the choke to loosen slightly.

As soon as the choke loosens, drop your chin down into the gap (to counter the choke as its reapplied) and at the same time, use the gap to start fighting back with one arm, whilst keeping the other hand pulling down on the attackers arm, until it is safe to remove it.

Defences Against Chokes & Strangulations

Chokes come in many shapes and forms, they can be double handed or single handed and use either the attackers hands or arm, as well as coming from the front, rear and sides.

Whilst chokes and strangles have similar effects, technically the difference between them is that a choke stops the oxygen travelling to your brain by cutting off your air supply by compressing the larynx, whilst a strangle cuts off your blood supply and thus oxygen levels by compressing the carotid arteries on either side of your neck. Whilst the terms are often used inter-changeably, the first course of action is always the same and essential, and that is to gain breathing room, because without doing so, your oxygen levels and thus your energy supply will dissipate quickly.

For training purposes, both chokes and strangles should be practiced with care and diligence.

Two Handed Front Strangle - Defence 1
For this defence, we use the grab and knee kick combination, first found in Toi-Gye tul.

1a, 1b & 1c. As the attacker starts to squeeze your neck, secure some breathing space by striking both palms down onto the attackers arms. This isn't designed to give a total release from the grip but just to take the pressure off your neck. At the same time, execute a knee kick to the attackers groin or stomach.

2. Follow the knee kick by stepping down with your right foot in front of the attackers, whilst at the same wrapping your arm around the opponents neck.

3a, 3b & 3c. Bring your opposite foot inline with your other foot and execute a hip throw to your opponent.

4. Once thrown, immediately drop your weight down onto the opponent via your knee.

Two Handed Front Strangle - Defence 2

For this defence, we use the combination found in Dan-Gun tul, consisting of a low outer forearm block, immediately followed by a outer forearm rising block.

1a, 1b & 1c. As the attacker grabs your throat, immediately execute the low outer forearm block to their elbow joints, grabbing their arm with your reaction hand. The aim here is to give you breathing space, as well as make the attacker bend forwards.

2. With the attacker bent forwards, execute the outer forearm rising block, upwards to the attackers jaw.

3. Follow up with strikes.

- The same defence can also be applied to a single handed choke attack.

Two Handed Front Strangle - Defence 3

For this defence, we use the combination found in Dan-Gun tul, consisting of a twin forearm block, followed by a high forefist punch.

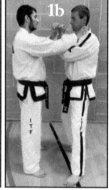

1a, 1b, 1c & 1d. As the attacker grabs your throat bring your arms inside theirs and execute the twin forearm block by striking both the attackers forearms with your own (ideally to their radial nerve) and continuing to execute the block by pushing forwards with your left arm (to their right arm) and upwards at an angle with your right arm (to their left arm), while at the same time, turning 90 degree's and dropping into your L-stance.

2. Grab onto the attackers right arm (with your left) and prepare to execute the high forefist punch. Do this even if one or both of the attackers grips have not released completely.

3a, 3b & 3c. Step forwards and execute the high punch behind the attackers head, so you actually strike them with your shoulder. Remembering to step forwards into a walking stance, as per the pattern.

4. You will find that you have easily executed a take-down, following which you can run away or chose to follow up on.

Two Handed Front Strangle - Defence 4

For this defence, we use a basic twisting motion to remove the attackers arms.

  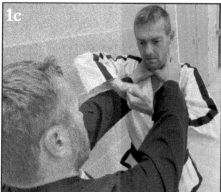

1a, 1b & 1c. As the attacker takes hold of your throat, bring your hands up and place one arm over the attackers arm and one arm under the attackers arm, locking your hands together in the middle.

2a & 2b. Twist your arms, so the one underneath goes upwards and the one on top is pressing downwards, onto the attackers arms.

3a & 3b. Once you have released from the strangle, follow

up with counter strikes.

Two Handed Front Strangle - Regaining Balance

Mounting any kind of defence is next to impossible if our equilibrium is disrupted, as the body will automatically look to regain balance first and foremost, above and beyond defending itself from a strike or any other attack. Nowhere is this more important than when being choked, as we have a limited time to defend against the choke before our body shuts down due to lack of oxygen, so its important to regain our balance quickly and we can do this by use of a simple sitting stance.

1a, 1b, 1c & 1d. As the attackers choke takes hold, they are also pushing us backwards at same time, making a defence impossible to mount, so we step back (as many times as needed), then pivot 90 degrees to form a sitting stance, side on to our opponent.

As the same time as we form our stance to regain our stability, we bring one arm over the attackers arms and trap them to our chest (using both hands) so we have control of our opponent.

2. With their hands trapped, we can immediately execute a side elbow strike, with the closest elbow to the opponents head.

3a & 3b. Following the side elbow strike, we grab hold of our opponent and follow up with a knee kick.

- Ankle Separation Follow Up

This technique can be used as a follow up to many counter attacks and is not so much a defence, but a counter-technique to finish a confrontation once and for all. I have made it as a separate section as its very dangerous to execute in training unless you do it properly and safely, which I shall explain on the next page. For now however, it flows from the previous techniques really well and it works like this:

4. Following the knee kick (3b), step your foot down directly onto the top of the attackers foot.

5. With out removing your foot, forcefully push the attacker backwards whilst keeping your weight firmly pressing down on the attackers foot, as this will separate their ankle joint, which means they wont be able to stand back up to continue an assault and will be in lots of pain!

When practicing this in class, ***do not*** keep your weight down on your training partners foot, you must lift it up as you push them, otherwise you will separate their ankle as well!

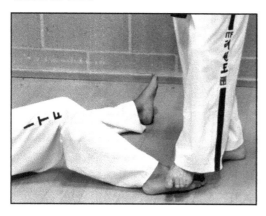 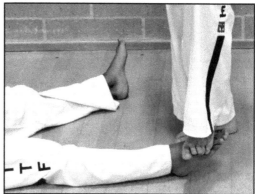

The reason this works so well is because it is impossible for most people to have their foot and their leg flat on the floor at the same time whilst lying flat on their back (see above pictures). If the foot is flat, the knee needs to be bent to compensate and if the leg is straight, then the foot needs to point up a bit.

In the defence, we trap the foot flat on the floor and by pushing the attacker backwards, lock their leg straight as well as they fall, as just with their initial attack on us, their body seeks to stabilize itself first and foremost, in this case its by landing safely on the floor and thus, doesn't even think about bending the leg or lifting the foot to protect their ankle.

Two Handed Rear Strangle - Defence 1
For this defence, we use a circular block, that we first find in Won-Hyo tul.

1a, 1b & 1c. As the attacker attempts a strangle from behind, spin around, raising one of your arms higher than the attackers, which will likely knock one of their arms to the side, releasing the strangulation attempt.

2a & 2b. As you spin around, loop your arm over and around both of the attackers arms, in

the circular block motion, ensuring it completely loops around the attackers arms. Press inwards to add some pain!

3. With the attackers arms wrapped up, counter-attack with your free hand.

Two Handed Rear Strangle - Defence 2

This defence is fairly simple and uses *'stepping forwards into walking stance'* with a back piercing kick follow up!

1a & 1b. As you feel the attackers hands on your neck, immediately step forwards sharply into a walking stance.

2a & 2b. Execute a back piercing kick to the attacker.

Rear Choke - Defence 1

For this defence, we use rear elbow strikes, followed by a palm pressing block, as seen in Joong-Gun tul, to escape and create an armlock.

1a & 1b. As the attackers arm wraps around your throat, secure your airway by cupping both hands and pulling down sharply on the attackers arms.

2a & 2b. Perform a rear elbow strike to the attackers ribs on the opposite side of the arm that's choking you. Keep striking until you create some space to manoeuvre.

3. Rotate towards the attacker using the space created by the elbow strikes. As you do so, bend forward and attempt to slip your head through the gap. Control the attackers arm to help you slip through by using your other arm to push on the attackers elbow as you slip through.

4. Once you are through, pull the attackers arm straight, whilst pressing down on their elbow joint (in palm pressing block motion) to create an arm lock or break the arm and follow up as required.

Rear Choke - Defence 2

To escape from this choke, we use a **rear elbow strike which allows us to slip out of the choke and counter attack.**

1a, 1b & 1c. As the attacker chokes you, grab hold of their arm and pull down sharply (to give you some breathing room), whilst at the same time elbowing their ribs with your other arm.

2. Ensure you attack their ribs on the side that they are using to choke you, because as you strike with your elbow, you immediately pivot towards the opponent, but also outwards, away from the choke.

3a & 3b. As soon as you slip out, follow up with counter strikes.

Rear Choke - Defence 3

For this escape, we use a **side elbow thrust, similar to the one we execute in Hwa-Rang tul.**

1a & 1b. As the attacker applies the choke, cup your hands and pull down sharply on the attackers arm, whilst applying a foot stamp (with your heel) to the top of the attackers foot.

2. The foot stamp should

create some space as the attacker reacts to the pain, so use this space to immediately elbow the attacker in the ribs with the point of your elbow.

3. The elbow strike to the ribs should create some more space as the attacker recoils from it and as soon as they do (which will be immediate), use the same elbow and throw it straight up behind you to the attackers jaw.

Rear Choke - Defence 4

For this defence we use a basic shoulder throw, plus an easier alternative for those who may not be so skilled at throwing techniques.

1a & 1b. As the choke is applied from behind, strike the attackers groin with one hand, then immediately reach back with your other hand, grabbing and gripping strongly onto the opponents clothes on their shoulder, while lowering your centre and bucking your hips backwards to break the opponents balance.

2a, 2b & 2c. Execute a shoulder throw by straightening your legs and pulling the attacker forwards, twisting at the last second to drop them in front of you.

3a & 3b. With the attacker thrown in front of you, finish with a stamping kick to the attackers body.

4a, 4b, 4c, 4d, 4e & 4f. Alternatively, for those who are not comfortable with standing shoulder throws, or to aid the student in throwing a much heavier opponent, you can execute the same throw, but kneeling as you do so, thus using gravity and your body weight more efficiently to help with the throw. If you look 'outside the box', this technique is actually found in Po-Eun tul *(see Ch'ang Hon Taekwon-do Hae Sul - Vol. 2).*

Side Headlock - Defence 1

To escape from this side headlock, we use the U-shape blocks found in Joong-Gun tul.

1a & 1b. As you are trapped in the side headlock raise your rear arm up and over the attackers head, whilst positioning your other arm near the rear of their knee.

2a & 2b. Grab onto the attackers hair, eye sockets or anything you can grab hold of.

3a, 3b & 3c Immediately pull the attackers head violently backwards (sharply), whilst at the same time using your other arc-hand to strike to the back of the attackers knee joint and continue by raising their front leg. Execute both in a circular motion.

4a & 4b. As the attacker falls to the ground, immediately follow up with counter strikes.

Side Headlock - Defence 2

For this escape, we use a painful grip and twist to the attackers inside thigh.

1a, 1b & 1c. As the attacker has you trapped in the side headlock, reach your lead arm around and grab the inside thigh of your opponent.

2a & 2b. Immediately squeeze and twist your grip, which creates a lot of pain in the attacker, loosening their grab.

3. As you twist the attackers thigh and the grip loosens, slip your head out of the side headlock.

4a & 4b. Counter strike to the back of the attackers head with a forearm smash or reverse knifehand.

Side Headlock - Defence 3
For this defence we use basic hook punches to secure our release.

1a, 1b, 1c & 1d. As you are trapped in the side headlock one of your arms is available at the front, with the other at the rear, so start by using a hook punch with your front arm to strike at the opponents abdomen.

2a, 2b & 2c. As soon as your first strike lands, immediately continue with a rear hook punch to the opponents kidneys.

3a, 3b & 3c. Continue to alternate your punches between front and rear strikes, in quick succession, until the attacker is forced to release the headlock (3c).

4a & 4b. As soon as you are released from the headlock, follow up by counter attacking the opponents head.

Side Headlock - Defence 4

For this defence we use a rear foot sweep, similar to the one found in Sam-Il tul.

1a, 1b & 1c. As the attacker applies the side headlock, grab their arm with your front hand and their shoulder with your rear hand.

2a, 2b, 2c, 2d & 2e. Whilst maintaining your grip on the attackers shoulder and arm, use your rear foot to execute a sweep to the back of the attackers leg and as you do so, pull the attackers shoulder backwards whilst also pulling on their gripping arm. The attackers natural instinct to regain balance will take over and they will release their grip as you sweep them over.

3a & 3b. Follow up with a foot stamp or simply run away.

Side Headlock (or Rear Choke) - Defence 5

This defence uses a basic breakfall roll (that all students learn before throwing techniques) to escape a side headlock. It can also be used to escape a rear choke (as many of these type of defences are interchangeable), if the student can manage to slip their body to the side of the attackers, thus forming the same side headlock position.

1a & 1b. As the side headlock is applied, use your front hand to strike the attacker in the groin, whilst bringing your rear hand up to the rear of the attackers neck.

2a & 2b. As soon as the groin strike connects, start rolling into the front breakfall and as you do so, push your striking hand into the opponents belly, whilst pulling him with you (forwards and downwards) by using your rear hand, as well as the momentum of the breakfall roll.

3a, 3b, 3c & 3d. As you roll, keep your arm locked as straight as possible in the attackers belly, which will help to throw the opponent over you, rather than bringing them down on top of you.

4a & 4b. With the opponent thrown, you could continue and roll further using the momentum and use your foot to kick the opponent whilst they are down to finish them off.

Front Guillotine Choke - Defence 1

For this defence, we use a number of basic striking techniques to secure our release.

1a & 1b. As the attacker starts to apply the front guillotine choke, grab the arm choking you with one arm and pull down for some breathing space, while at the same time executing a reverse knifehand strike to the attackers groin.

2. As the attacker naturally leans forwards due to the groin strike, bring your striking arm straight up, executing an upwards elbow strike to the attackers jaw.

3a & 3b. As the attacker reacts to the elbow strike, their choke will have loosened, so pull your head out of it and strike with an arc-hand to their throat.

Front Guillotine Choke - Defence 2

For this defence, we use a knee kick to enable our escape.

1a & 1b. As the front guillotine choke is applied, grab (or cup) the attackers choking arm and pull down sharply, dropping your body weight at the same time.

2a & 2b. As soon as you gain some breathing room, place one hand (on the opposite side to the choke) over the attackers shoulder and use your other hand to grab the clothing on their leg.

3. With your hands in position, manoeuvre yourself to the side of the attacker. Your own grabs will stop the attacker being able to turn with you.

4a, 4b & 4c. From your side on position, execute a knee strike to either the attackers thigh or the side of their knee (*4a*).

Alternatively, if you were able to get a bit further round, you may be able to attack the back of the attackers knee and take them down from there (*4b and 4c*).

Front Guillotine Choke - Defence 3

To escape from this choke, we use the U-shape block found in Joong-Gun tul. If executed slowly, it will require some strength, but as long as the opponent isn't overly heavy, when executed quickly it works using unbalancing and momentum.

1a & 1b. As the opponent places you in the choke, execute your u-shape block, placing one arm over the attackers shoulder and the other between his legs.

2a & 2b. The next part of this defence is just like in the pattern (Joong-Gun), where you change from one u-shape block to the other - Bring the arm between the attackers legs upwards (pressing on his thigh), whilst lowering your other arm, which will rotate the attacker.

3a & 3b. As you flip the attacker over, let go of their upper body, that you had in your other arm, so they get dropped, head first, onto the ground.

4a & 4b. Finish off the attacker with a foot stamp.

Front Guillotine Choke - Defence 4

This defence uses the 180 degree stepping motions that we find in Ge-Baek tul.

1a & 1b. As the front guillotine choke is applied and the attacker starts to pull upwards, grab their arm with both hands and pull sharply downwards whilst dropping your body weight at the same time. This will give you some breathing room, by removing some of the pressure from your throat and hopefully enough room to manoeuvre into the next part of the defence.

2a & 2b. You should now have some room to manoeuvre (due to the pulling down of the opponents arm), so start to move out of the attackers choke by stepping your closest leg (to the attacker), forwards and to the side of them, whilst rotating your body 90 degree's. Try to lean forwards a bit, keeping a grip on the opponents arm as you step through.

3. Complete the turn by bringing your other leg forwards, between your own leg and the attackers leg, whilst turning a further 90 degrees, still holding the attackers arm.

4. As you finalize your turn, slip your palm on top of the attackers elbow joint and press downwards, to form an armlock.

5. Finish up with a knee strike to the attackers head.

Single Handed Front Strangle - Defence 1

These defences are at the end of the Chokes and Strangles chapter because to be honest they are very simple to avoid (by stepping backwards) and even if not, they are just as simple to escape from. Unless the grip is really really strong around your throat, you can just step backwards and pull your throat out of the choke. However, as some students may panic, it is still useful to know a few defences against them

1a, 1b & 1c. As the attacker grabs your throat immediately grab their arm with both hands and simultaneously execute a front snap kick between their legs. Leaning back slightly as you do so takes away some of the threat from a possible follow up punch, as well as initiates the release as you strike home with your kick.

Single Handed Front Strangle - Defence 2

This defence uses the motion of the outer forearm downward block found in Juche and Ko-Dang tul.

1a & 1b. As the strangle is applied by the attacker, grab their wrist (on the inside) with one hand as this will help alleviate the pressure of the strangle, whilst bringing your other arm, up and to the outside of the attackers.

2a & 2b. Execute the outer forearm downward block to the top and side of the attackers elbow joint, keeping your grip on the attackers wrist as you do so. Pivot as you execute the block.

The downward motion will both remove the attackers strangle and bend their arm, pulling him forwards as you pivot.

3a & 3b. Turn as much as needed to bring the attacker into the bent over position, whilst maintaining your grip on their wrist and then execute a downward elbow strike to the back of the attackers neck or spine.

Single Handed Front Strangle - Defence 3

This is a very simple defence and uses a flat fingertip thrust that we first find in Toi-Gye tul.

1a, 1b & 1c. As the attacker grabs your throat, cup your hand and strike down on their forearm to ease the strangle. At the same time, thrust your fingers into the opponents eyes. Alternatively you could palm strike their nose or jaw.

Biting Fighting

Along with the twisting of soft tissue to cause pain *(see the Side Headlock - Defence 2)*, one very much overlooked area is biting. A bite causes a reaction and can often facilitate part of a release, often giving that all important 'wiggle room'. In actual self-defence you would bite as hard as you can, aiming to rip into any soft tissue area of the attacker that you can clamp your teeth on.

In training however, you can still bite, but you bite just enough to get a reaction but not hard enough to break the skin, sometimes this may even leave tooth marks, but it will give students a new Hosinsul tool in their defence toolbox that they may never have considered before.

Bite Defence against a choke or a strangle

The jaw muscles are some of the most powerful muscles in our body and our teeth are one of our sharpest tools. As martial artists we often trim our nails for training (which can be another good weapon), but our teeth remain hard and sharp and when coupled with those powerful jaw muscles, can make a formidable weapon for us to use, if applicable.

Bite Defence against a guillotine choke

Biting is probably most applicable to this section (Defences Against Chokes & Strangles), as the defenders head is often close to the attackers body or limbs, but it should also be considered as a self defence technique in other areas, for example if you are grabbed, sinking your teeth into the attackers arm may facilitate a release or give you some precious seconds for a follow up.

"Where there is only a choice between cowardice and violence,
I would advise violence."

- *Mahatma Gandhi*

Chapter 7
Defences Against 'Other' Attacks

Defences Against Headbutts

Headbutts are very dangerous attacks, usually catching the unsuspecting student by complete surprise. Ideally, an attacker should never get close enough to execute a headbutt if we use a fence properly. Headbutts can be executed with or without a grab first, but the most common is a front headbutt executed just after a double lapel grab which ensures the victim is both within range of the headbutt and gives the attacker extra force by pulling himself into the attacker.

Unfortunately most students rarely practice headbutts in class, which is a shame as not only is practicing them easy to do (with focus pads), it also means students will rarely consider them as counter techniques, or if they do, they won't know how to use them. More so, some instructors will actively discourage headbutt techniques because they are unsportsmanlike , but self defence isn't a sport! The use of headbutts is also considered unladylike, which means they become an even more unsuspected counter-attack when used by a female!

Whilst the most common headbutt is executed from the front, there are also rear headbutts and side headbutts and the general rule with all types of headbutts is the *'eye brows'*. What this means is that you use your eye brows as your guide to headbutting; if you execute one, you do so by hitting with your head above your eye brow line, whilst attacking (or counter-attacking in our case), the opponents head below their eye brow line.

Headbutt - Defence 1
This defence utilizes the 'Heaven Hand' position found in Kwang-Gae tul and Po-Eun tul.

1a, 1b & 1c. As the attacker grabs hold of you, bring both hands straight up in the inside of the attackers arm, forming the heaven hand position, whilst tilting your head down.

If we are quick enough we can block the headbutt, if slightly slower we can at least place a cushion between the headbutt and our own head.

2a & 2b. Once the headbutt has been nullified, with our own arms inside of the attackers, we can turn our heaven hand into an elbow strike, simply by bending our arm and pivoting into the strike with a turning elbow.

Headbutt - Defence 2

This is a basic defence, that can be utilised quickly, when you have very limited reaction time.

1a, 1b & 1c. As the attacker grabs hold of you and tries to headbutt you, tilt your head forwards (while clenching your teeth) and take the headbutt on the top of your head.

It will hurt a bit, but a lot less than if you took it in your face.

2. Whilst the attacker is surprised and has both hands gripped on you, execute a knee kick to the groin, then follow up with other strikes, releases or locks.

Handshake With Intent

Although a handshake isn't often considered a technique you need a defence against, I have included some options in this book on how to deal with them, as often the handshake is a precursor to a strike, a pull or a grab (to take you into a side headlock for example), if there is intent behind it.

By grabbing your hand in a handshake, an attacker not only has control of one of your arms, making it hard to block a follow up punch, but also lowers your mental guard making your reaction times slower. Here we look at a couple of ways to deal with such a situation, which ideally, you should anticipate and be prepared for.

Handshake With Intent - Defence 1

This is a way to turn a handshake into an armlock, and requires the student to use his arms to form close ready stance 'C', that is the ready posture for Hwa-Rang tul.

1a, 1b & 1c. As you shake hands with the attacker, pivot to the outside, whilst wrapping your other arm over the attackers.

2a & 2b. Keeping hold of the attackers hand, continue wrapping your arm around the attackers by bringing it underneath their arm and onto the back of your own arm.

3a & 3b. At this point the attackers arm should be locked with its palm up and you can apply further pressure by raising your

body upwards i.e. Forming the close stance.

Handshake With Intent - Defence 2

This defence to a handshake with intent, uses the twin horizontal punch that 1st degrees will recognise from Po-Eun tul, to turn into a locking technique, which can either break the attackers arm or be used as a 'come along' hold.

1a, 1b & 1c. Take hold of the attackers arm via the handshake and pull it towards you whilst placing your other arm underneath the attackers arm.

2a & 2b. Grab onto the attackers clothing with your other arm and pivot slightly to form the twin horizontal punch, fully locking the attackers arm in the process.

Rugby Style Front Tackle
AKA Double Leg Takedown

A rugby style front tackle is a dangerous attack, that takes the defender by surprise, dumping them on the ground leaving them very vulnerable to the aggressors follow ups, which is usually a load of punches to the victims head! In grappling martial arts, this attack, in its more stylised form is called a *'Double Leg Take Down'*.

Rugby Style Front Tackle - Defence 1

This defence is one of the few in this book that isn't a part of the standard Taekwon-Do arsenal of techniques, however, its such an important defence, that all martial artists should know, to stop themselves being taken to the floor, which is why it is included here. Ironically, Taekwon-Do does actually have a slightly more stylized version of 'the sprawl', as it is known in Jiu-Jitsu and MMA circles.

1a, 1b & 1c. As the opponent moves towards you, attempting to wrap their arms around your thighs in order to execute a rugby style tackle (known as a double leg takedown to martial artists), swiftly jump backwards, moving both feet, arching your body and drop fully onto the opponents back.

2a & 2b. Use both your body weight, coupled with the momentum of dropping downwards, to force the opponent to the ground. Open your legs wide as you do so, so they cannot grab your legs.

3. At this stage, most grappling arts will continue by using ground based grappling techniques, but unless you are well versed in them, it's a good idea to strike and run whilst we have the advantage and we do this by executing a knee strike to the opponents head.

Rugby Style Front Tackle - Defence 2
This defence is actually found in the 2nd degree pattern Eui-Am tul and is the more stylised version of the sprawl. The technique we use is the twin palm downward block, that is seen in the second half of Eui-Am.

1a, 1b &1c. As the attacker attempts to take us down with a rugby style tackle to our legs, we shift our legs backwards, out of range of the attempted tackle and as the opponent over-reaches, execute the twin palm downward block to the opponents back, pressing down towards the ground.

Note: In the pattern Eui-Am, we just shift our front foot backwards to form the rear foot stance when executing the twin palm downward block, but in reality, it is highly advisable to shift both feet backwards.

2a & 2b. With the opponent on the floor, we can follow up with a stamping kick or a front snap kick or better still, in a real situation, just run!

Rugby Style Front Tackle - Defence 3

It is often said that 'sometimes the best defence is a good offence' and that is the case with this defence, where we use an **upper elbow strike**, that we first find in Joong-Gun tul.

1a & 1b. As the attacker moves in to try to take you to the floor with a double leg takedown, step forwards towards the attack.

2. As you step forwards, execute an upper elbow strike, aiming to 'check' the opponent with it on either one of their shoulders. If you misjudge it, then you will have struck them in the face or head anyway (so be careful in training).

3. Immediately follow up. Here I use a a turning elbow strike with my other arm, as the body mechanics work well.

Rugby Style Front Tackle - Defence 4

While this defence takes some practice to master, it is highly useful to know, as unlike the other defences so far, it works when the double leg take down has taken hold and you are already being lifted off the ground. Whilst it may look complicated, in actual fact it simply uses a rear breakfall roll!

1a & 1b. As the attacker takes hold and lifts you off your feet with their double leg takedown, grab hold of their clothing and allow yourself to be taken down.

2a & 2b. As you fall backwards, use the momentum of the takedown (and gravity) to pull your attacker down with you. At the same time, try to slip one of your feet between the attackers legs and hook it behind.

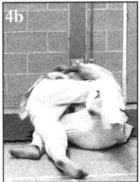

3a, 3b & 3c. Continue rolling backwards whilst at the same time using the leg you hooked around the opponents leg to roll them over further, by pushing it upwards.

4a, 4b & 4c. Using the momentum of the roll, as you throw the opponent over you, continue rolling backwards and you will end up on top of your stunned opponent.

5a, 5b, 5c & 5d. With the advantage now yours, start striking your opponent with your fists.

6a, 6b & 6c. Finally, to get up and off your opponent, strike down with both palms hard to their chest, pushing yourself up and off them at the same time. **DO NOT** do this hard in training.

"Force has no place where there is need of skill"

- Herodotus

Chapter 8
Advanced Hosinsul

Advanced Hosinsul

In the main, formal Hosinsul training within a Taekwon-Do class, usually involves one student attacking and one student defending and counter-attacking. But, an instructor can take the standard practice a bit further, in a number of ways, to cover more than one on one attacks.

More Than A Single Attack

These are advanced versions of Hosinsul between two students and there are a number of ways you can practice.

Multiple Attacks - You can allow multiple attacks, meaning the attacking student can, for example throw a punch, followed by another punch with the opposite hand or can grab and follow that up with a strike. This means a student has to deal with varying circumstances and can't solely focus on the first technique that is thrown at them, they have to adapt.

Weak Grip Releases - One thing you sometimes see with the defending student is weak grips when they are counter-attacking. For example, they have intercepted an incoming strike and then weakly hold the attackers arm, whilst they throw a counter technique with their other hand. In reality this wouldn't work so well, as the attacker could pull their arm away and throw another attack with it, so when training, if the attacker feels their arm isn't secured by the defender, they are allowed to point that out, either by pulling it away and simply using it again or to highlight it, pull it away and give the defender a light slap around their head to let them know.

Resisting Attackers - This allows the attacker to resist the defences. Hosinsul should be instantaneous following the initial attack, but sometimes students seem to take a bit too long, but the attacker allows them to get on with it none the less. In reality this wouldn't work, so the idea here is that after the attacker has attacked, they count "1, 2" (in their head) and then can throw another technique, or pull their arm away, turn a choke into a throw of their own or do what ever else the instructor deems appropriate.

The Attacker Is The Defender - This training method works like this: The attacker attacks as per standard Hosinsul, and the defending student defends and counters. Once the defending student initiates their counter-attack, the original attacking student is allowed to defend themselves.

Street Clothes - Training Hosinsul in clothes, often puts a different take on things than doing so in standard doboks. For a start we are wearing shoes or trainers, which help with kicks. Tight jeans can cause problems, T-shirts present issues not apparent when training in long sleeved doboks and we can often pull jumpers over the opponents head, to cover their vision. Training in normal clothes is a very good method of practice and on occasion I simply tell students not to get changed into their doboks when they arrive at class, so they train in something they would wear everyday (as opposed to tracksuits or other clothing designed for ease of movement). Of course, this type of training, when done unaware, has it limits, as no one wants their expensive top damaged, but it does show students the importance of thinking about what they wear, in case they ever have to defend themselves for real!

Dim Light and Darkness - Another training method to consider is to turn the lights down or off altogether, so students get used to defending themselves in low light. At first, it is very hard to see, as everyone's eyes adjust to the darkness, but eventually it gets easier, though everything is just a little bit harder in these circumstances.

All of the above are variations on what you would do in class normally, of course it goes without saying that they should only be practiced with permission of the instructor (if in class) and of course with the full agreement of both students, so they know exactly what is going on.

Other (Advanced) Area's Of Hosinsul

For those that have studied the training of Hosinsul and how it is practiced within Taekwon-Do, there is also the practice of Hosinsul *seated* (in a chair with the attacker opposite you, in a chair with the attacker next to you and cross legged on the ground), *kneeling* and *prone* (lying on the ground). General Choi's manual also cover some defences against *weapons* (knives, bayonets, clubs and he even touches upon pistol defences).

Weapons Defence

Though defences against weapons appear in General Choi's 15 volumes, many of the defences displayed are either outdated or even dangerous in my opinion. Weapons defence should be considered a specialised area of Hosinsul and thus, for the instructor who wishes to teach it, requires an expert with more knowledge in this area than your average Taekwon-Do instructor or even Master.

I teach weapon defences at my Academy, including defences against knives, clubs (short stick), poles and even pistols, however the techniques and tactics I teach to deal with such weapons are not the standard material you see in many martial arts books. They were learnt via in-depth instruction by a military unarmed combat instructor, as well as a LEO (Law Enforcement Officer, who also wrote a manual on dealing with weapons for prison officers in his county in the US - he is also ex-military as well) and I would recommend anybody who wants to incorporate this area of Hosinsul into their school or training to seek out someone with that type of knowledge and experience in order to plug this gap effectively.

Teaching Knife Defences at a Seminar in Scotland, 2014

Seated Hosinsul

This is also an area of training that we cover at my school with the black belts, when they practice Hosinsul. However, in my opinion, its range of defences are not that different from standing Hosinsul. As long as you can nullify the original attack (often in the same or a similar way that you would if standing), then the defender can stand up from the chair and continue their counter attack.. It is fairly easy to incorporate as long as some safety precautions are applied, such as placing mats around the chairs in case the defender is knocked backwards.

One version of Seated Hosinsul, with the students sitting opposite each other.

Another version of Seated Hosinsul, with the students sitting next to each other.

Following the defence of the initial attack, an armlock is put on the aggressor

Prone Hosinsul

Prone Hosinsul refers to the student having to defend themselves whilst lying on the ground against a standing attacker, The basic tactic in Taekwon-Do is to kick or strike to the standing attacker, whilst still lying on the ground.

Of course, you can practice striking off the ground, to focus pads and kick shields, but you will find that it's not that easy as it's hard to gain a lot of power when striking upwards whilst lying on the floor. In my opinion, it would be better to spend such practice time working on keeping the opponent at bay, so they cannot strike, kick or grab you whilst you are on the your back.

Prone Defence - Method 1

If you are on your back, with an attacker still standing, you can use the following method to keep them at bay, until the opportunity presents itself to get back on your feet.

As you go down, stay on your back and keep your feet in the direction of the attacker. Each time the attacker moves in to kick, strike or grab you, sharply kick out at them, over and over until they back away.

As they try to move around you, to get past your defence (your kicking feet), swivel around on your lower back or backside, to keep your feet (and thus kicks) between you and the attacker.

When you kick out, kick quickly and sharply. The defending student isn't aiming for a particular place, just kick wildly. If you manage to injure the attacker, or hit them hard enough that they step back far enough, in a real situation, that would be your opportunity to get back onto your feet.

In training, set a time limit, in which the defender has to successfully keep the defender at bay for a set period of time.

Prone Defence - Method 2

This method takes into account the fact that the defender is on the ground and the attacker may be too close already to place themselves in the position shown in method 1.

With yourself on the ground and the attacker still standing, roll onto your side and cover by bringing your knees up and placing your forearms in front. The knees are to protect your lower body and your arms to protect your head and upper body.

In class, the students should practice covering, taking shots on the arms and legs and swivelling around as the opponent tries to bypass their guard. If the opportunity presents itself to kick out at the attacker or to grab the attackers foot, then do so, but the main aim here it to cover against incoming blows until you can get back on your feet.

Prone Defence - Regaining Your feet

Of course, apart from defending ourselves, we should look to get back on our feet as soon as possible, as inevitably it will be hard to maintain such defences, so we should always keep that in mind.

As you have seen, defending on the ground with our legs is preferable, as they are stronger and harder to grab than our arms and even untargeted, can do considerably more damage to a standing opponent, whilst we are prone.

So if you manage to strike the opponent and create a gap, then that is the time to regain your standing posture, so you can better defend yourself or in a real situation, run.

If, whilst defending, we manage to throw a kick and strike the attacker hard enough to create a gap, use that time to stand up before the attacker recovers enough to continue their attack.

In this scenario, we have managed to get a kick to the attackers leg, which has hurt them enough to make them pause and momentarily move backwards a bit.

As they do so, we shift back quickly, to create a bigger gap between the attacker and us, then quickly go onto one knee, prior to standing up fully.

We go onto one knee, rather than using both our hands to push us straight up, as if we do that, both our hands and arms are momentarily engaged with helping to lift us off the floor and cannot be used to defend ourselves should the

attacker engage us again. We can often get onto one knee, without using our hands/arms at all, or simply using one, which means we can maintain a defence throughout.

Once up, prepare to fight or run!

Fighting On The Ground

Whilst 'Prone Hosinsul' is the practice of the defender on the ground, while the attacker is still upright, often in real life both the defender and attacker will end up on the ground together and this is where some outside instruction will be of benefit.

Unfortunately, in the early days of Taekwon-Do (and even now), a fallacy was put forwards that a student of Taekwon-Do would rarely, if ever, find themselves on the ground, due to their fast footwork and lighting quick reflexes, with blows that would stop an attacker with one strike. In reality, this is not the case, so we are left with a weak link in our Taekwon-Do arsenal.

Fighting on the ground, without some prior training is not productive at all and often leaves the two students just flailing around, not really knowing what to do. We have to consider this is a major weak point within our system and that there are other martial arts (such as Judo, Brazilian Jiu-Jitsu etc.) that are much better at groundwork than Taekwon-Do will ever be, simply as it's a major part of their arts and something they are able to practice at every single class, so it may be better to simply ask a Judo instructor (for example), to show you a few decent ground techniques that you can incorporate into your regular training.

In lieu of some extra training by an expert in this field, one strategy to employ (and thus train regularly), is to get back on your feet as soon as possible. Of course, one thing all students need to learn is how to get an opponent, who is sitting on top of them off, giving an opportunity to get back on your feet or at least not be overpowered whilst on the ground.

Removing An Opponent Sitting On Top (Choke)

There are many ways to remove an opponent who is sitting on top of you, using their bodyweight to keep you down. Defences can vary depending on their (sitting) position and what they are doing. For example pinning your arms down, striking you or in this example, choking you.

As the opponent is on top of you and trying to choke you, you must act quickly.

1a & 1b. From your initial position underneath, draw your knee's up and try to put one foot to the outside of the opponents leg, to act as a hinge point for when you initiate the release. Place it over the leg on the side you wish to roll the opponent to. The other leg will be used to push up from the floor once the release is in motion.

2a & 2b. As you draw you knee's up, almost immediately cup one hand (on the same side as your foot is placed over the opponents leg) and sharply hit (and pull)

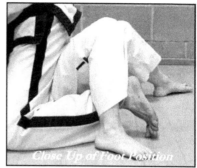

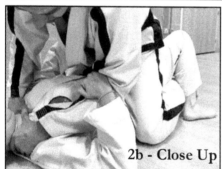

2b - Close Up

downwards to the inside of the opponents elbow joint - the aim is to bend it downwards, breaking the opponents balance.

At the same time, push up on the opponents body (stomach area) firmly with your other hand and also push up your opposite hip with your other leg, turning your whole body to the side.

2b - Top View

3. Continue pushing with both your leg and your hand to roll the opponent off you to the side.

4a, 4b & 4c. Continue the momentum of the roll and you should find yourself on top of the attacker. Immediately rain punches down to their face (or in this case, their throat).

Removing An Opponent Sitting On Top (Pin)

If the opponent is sitting on top of you and pinning your arms to the ground, you need to use your legs and hips to remove them, but also a bit of trickery.

1a & 1b. With your arms pinned and the opponent sitting all their weight on top of you, draw your knees up, whilst at the same time fake that you are trying to escape or resist by pushing your arms up as well - this is the trickery part and will hide your real intentions, as well as aid the escape technique.

2a & 2b. At the same time, relax your arms and buck your hips forcefully upwards, pushing sharply off the floor with your feet. These motions combined, if done violently enough should throw your opponent forwards, and off you.

3a & 3b. Whilst the opponent adjusts to their dilemma, use the time to stand up and prepare to run or fight. If they haven't come fully off you, wiggle backwards quickly before they realise what is happening.

Dealing With An Opponent On Top (Striking)

An opponent sitting on top and punching down at you, is a dangerous position to be in, so you must act quickly.

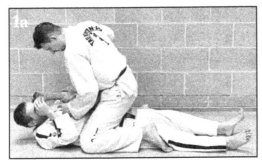

1a, 1b & 1c. As the opponent starts striking at your face, your initial instinct will be to cover up *(1b)*, but don't let the punches rain down on you! Almost immediately, you need to reach up and grab the opponents head or neck.

2. Pull the opponent sharply downwards into you, ensuring you pull them towards your shoulder and not your face. This will nullify their strikes.

3a & 3b. With the opponent close to you, immediately start to strike them, using punches or in this case, elbow strikes.

Choke Sparring

Whilst in-depth ground fighting is beyond the scope of this book, it is clear that some consideration was given to what to do if you find yourself being attacked whilst on the ground, but it remains one of the few weak areas in Taekwon-Do until it is addressed.

One way to do this is by a training method we, at my Taekwon-Do Academy, call Choke Sparring and the concept is simple. If both the defender and attacker find themselves on the floor, rather than flailing around hoping for a solid strike or trying to get up, the quickest option is to go straight in and apply a choke to the aggressor.

Within 6 to 10 seconds, a good choke (or strangle) will render the opponent unconscious, allowing the student to stand up and get away.

With training, a choke will become the immediate go to option should you end up on the ground with your opponent, making it likely you can apply one before your opponent even has a chance to defend against it, as their thought process would likely be to try striking you or to try and get back up - you have one chance, get that choke on!

What's good about this training method is that many students already learnt a few standing chokes ready for standard Hosinsul anyway, so they just have to practice how to apply them on the ground. Coupled with applying the chokes, I also teach a few basics like how to turn an opponent whilst kneeling, what a sleeper hold is and

A Choke Sparring session at Rayners Lane Taekwon-do Academy (Circa 2006)

how to apply it etc.

We practice all the above from kneeling or lying positions, then we let them spar. In its most basic form, no striking is allowed as this allows the students to purely concentrate on getting their chokes on or defending against them. More advanced forms may include allowing strikes, armbars, ankle locks and other techniques.

Students start off sitting back to back, with their legs straight out, so no student has an advantage. Upon the call of 'Sijak' (begin), both students turn (no standing up is allowed) and attempt to place a choke on the other. All this is watched by a third person for safety. A double tap is used to signal a choke is on well or the 3rd person will continually check they are both okay and break them up should anything look dangerous, as sometimes a student cannot tap due to positioning.

I tell my students that there are two ways to win at Choke Sparring - choke your partner out and don't be choked out! Of course, this is a training method, so everybody wins, if everyone trains hard and gains something from it, as with Traditional Sparring the real aim it to be better able to defend yourself.

Whilst Choke Sparring is more in the realms of actual sparring/fighting, rather than

Following 'sijak' students start to grapple to find a way in to execute their chokes or strangles. In this example, the student on the right has managed to move around the opponent, place their strangle technique and execute a sleeper hold.
- the opponent double taps in the last picture.

Hosinsul per se, it is a good way to address the weak area of groundwork that Taekwon-Do has.

Multiple Attackers

A final area to consider incorporating into Hosinsul training is how to deal with more than one aggressor. Unlike the movies, attackers do not wait whilst you defend against the first one before they attack, however, with that said, there is usually an instigator (the one who throws the first punch) and that punch is often the catalyst for all the others to join in. Even for a highly trained fighter, trying to take on two or three attackers at close range is extremely difficult and by far the best strategy to employ is to be pre-emptive and attack first!

Training methods on how to deal with multiple attackers can take a number of different formats, but the first thing students should learn about is the 'pincer movement' and how to stop it happening. A pincer movement involves two or more aggressors and whilst one (in a real situation) would keep the student occupied, by talking to them or being aggressive towards them, another attacker would manoeuvre around the outside, often to the rear of the student, then grab them from behind, while the attacker at the front piles in. One effect of a rush of adrenaline into a students body is tunnel vision and when you couple that with the distraction taking place, by one of the aggressors, its easy to understand how an opponent is able to swiftly manoeuvre behind without you seeing them, even though they are right next to you.

How A Pincer Movement Works

1. The student is engaged and distracted by one of the aggressors.

2 & 3. Whilst the student is distracted, the other aggressor quickly moves around to be behind the student.

4 & 5. The student is caught in the pincer movement, between the two aggressors and surprised when one grabs them from behind, allowing the other one to attack from the front.

To avoid a pincer movement, it is vital to move your head a bit, to look from side to side so as to keep both opponents in your field of view, use of the fence is vital and should the aggressors try to pincer you, manoeuvre round, via stepping, whilst using the fence, so as not to allow any opponent out of your sight or to move to your side or behind you.

As I said, possibly the best option in a real situation is a pre-emptive strike, so in training we need to replicate that. However, the idea behind a pre-emptive strike to a group of multiple aggressors isn't to attack one of them and then use that advantage and continue to fight them, as we would a single aggressor, as this would allow the others to attack you whilst your engaged.

Instead, the idea is to strike one of the attackers as hard and as devastatingly as you can, then immediately switch and move onto another one of the aggressors. If there are more than two, you will need to only throw one or two strikes to the second aggressor, before moving to another or even back to the first one Of course this should be executed with surprise, speed, aggression and intent. By pre-emptively attacking with this method, there are a number of things we hope will happen:

1. The first opponent is taken out fully with your initial strike or if not, injured enough to not want to continue. At the very least it should take them by surprise, giving you some extra needed seconds to take the fight to the others.

2. The other aggressors may also be surprised by the pre-emptive attack, leaving them momentarily stunned at the very least, again giving you those extra precious seconds.

3. Seeing a fellow aggressor taken out, bleeding or injured should induce an adrenaline rush in the opponents, which hopefully they will mistake as fear and it may take the fight right out of them, leaving you with less or even no extra attackers to take on.

4. In all cases, at the very least it gives you a slight advantage.

However, all the above is for a real situation and we need to train as close to that as possible, in the dojang, whilst avoiding serious injuries to our training partners. In my school we start this process by using focus pads.

In the scenario above, we have two students (the aggressors) holding a set of focus pads each. They do not know who I will attack first, just that I will attack.. The pictures show I decide its my best option to go for the biggest and strongest of the two, as he will be more problematic to deal with later on and seeing the biggest guy get taken out will hopefully instil a lot of fear in his fellow aggressor! So I throw a hard right cross at at the biggest aggressor, then immediately switch and throw punches at the second aggressor. If we were to continue I would switch back to the first aggressor or drive through further into the second attacker, working on the basis of whether the first aggressor was or wasn't taken out of the fight, depending on which scenario I wish to drill.

Other scenarios would involve one or both of my training partners working to blind side me, by executing a pincer movement, forcing me to stop that and attack when I felt it was the right time.

Of course, many schools practice '2 Vs 1' Sparring, some even practice '3 Vs 1' and '4 Vs 1' Sparring as well, all of which have different tactics. However, these start at long range, not close range and usually, no grabbing is allowed either, meaning it ends up more of a fitness exercise, with some additional benefits if you employ and practice the correct tactics for each.

We do however need to incorporate some free movement into this form of training and we can start this by keeping all the contact light, but allowing things like grabs, pushes and takedowns, just like Traditional Sparring. Gradually we can build up contact levels, however, pitting two skilful students against each other is still not the same as a real situation, as they will know each other, have respect for each other and so won't wish to hurt each other and they will hold back a bit. Plus we lack any element of surprise.

More often than not, eventually the two aggressors will overcome the defender, take them to the ground or hold them whilst the other attacks, but if you look at it from the same perspective as Traditional Sparring - its all about the training, learning things, resisting things and dealing with situations, with no winners or losers - then you will get many benefits from it, that will help should you ever face this situation for real.

In the scenario above, I am fighting two aggressors (1) and the smallest one attacks quicker than the taller one, so I execute a quick side kick to his ribs (2) and then follow up with some punches (3) and try to finish him off with a knee kick. (4)

However, what I should of done is, after the kick or the punches, repositioned myself, as whilst I am engaged, the other aggressor has moved in to help his friend

(4) and grabbed me from behind (5). Whilst I try to escape the grab with a rear elbow strike (6), I have placed myself in a tough situation as the first aggressor may recover before I can escape the rear attack, leaving me in the middle of the two of them as well as being held from behind - next time I wont make the same mistake, as its all about learning and improving!

One option to use is a time limit. In training we are restricted on space, so you could mark out an area in which the student has to defend himself for a limited amount of time and when that time is up, they can escape by running out of the area, indicating an initial successful defence and running away.

Other variations on this type of training, are starting from a grabbed position or not allowing a defence until the attacker has initiated the attack with a first strike. We can even start with the defender on the ground, as if they have been pulled down first.

Related Study

Whilst standard Hosinsul is the basic training of 'body protection techniques', with some advanced variations, it is of course meant to be Dojang based training for realistic street attacks, so there is more that a student should know beyond just the physical defences.

Though it can't really be trained in class, I often mention to my students about scratching the attacker, not so much as a self defence technique, but so as to gather DNA underneath their fingertips, to be used to identify the perpetrator of the attack or crime.

I have already mentioned about understanding the law and how it works in regards to self defence, but I would also go further and discuss what reasonable force constitutes, in what scenario's a pre-emptive strike is allowed and what steps to take to ensure you don't fall foul of the law (such as stepping backwards, saying you don't want any trouble etc.), line up and trigger techniques, how a knock out works, avoiding sucker punches, how the best defence against weapons is to run, really fast, if you can and if not, to create a barrier between you and the attacker (such as a bag or dustbin lid for example), use a weapon of your own if viable, with the last resort being empty handed defence against them, especially knives and other edged weapons! With this in mind some basic street first aid advice might be good, including what to do if you are stabbed or slashed. A discussion about incidental weapons (items such as car keys, mobile phones, pens etc.) and their uses, if needed, as most students do not consider such things.

Talking (and training) regarding visual awareness (of your surroundings) is always a good idea, plus some basic safety tips such a not walking around with your head stuck in a mobile phone, checking inside your car before getting in, not taking dangerous shortcuts in the dark and similar tips always prove useful, as is the notion of shouting fire! instead of help! as passersby are less fearful of seeing what's going on when fire! is shouted and an assailant simply being spotted could often end an attack.

On the physical side, a discussion of how adrenaline works and how it affects the body is a good idea, accompanied with a discussion on fight or flight response, the effects of fear and what I call 'lessons in aggression' or how to get into fight mode quickly. Some study and practice of verbal de-escalation techniques may also prove useful.

Of course, teaching vital points is a must and should be part of standard classes anyway, but going a bit further and discussing the cause and effect of vital points, when hit, is a good idea too, for example, many students think that poking their fingers at an attackers eye may blind them, which it might, but its more likely to hurt and shock them a little, giving you a few seconds escape time, knowing this may make a student less likely to err on the side of caution and do what's needed should they be attacked for real. I often present students with a worst case and more likely scenarios when discussing certain techniques and vital point strikes.

If you run adult classes you could take training one step further and add in verbal abuse to the proceedings, as this can often shock people when it is used against them for real, as many aren't use to people swearing, verbally abusing and threatening them and in a real situation could cause them to freeze.

A little chat about pride, ego and the consequences of violence, especially with younger male students can prove useful. I often explain to them that its always better to walk away from trouble where possible, as apart from the physical injuries that could happen to them, especially if they do not come out on top, should the worst happen, such as they are crippled, blinded or killed, then there is an emotional side that will affect everyone that loves them - mum, dad, sisters, brothers, their children, other family members and friends. And of course, even if you do come out on top, the same things may happen to your attacker, which you will have to carry with you for the rest of your life, so you have to ask yourself, even if it wasn't your fault, as to why it started, is it really worth taking it forwards, if you don't have to or is the contents of your wallet or your mobile phone really comparable to the cost of your life!

For all age groups, appropriate scenario based training is another avenue to explore, this can be structured towards specific age groups, with situations that happen more often, such as young adult males and arguments (incidents at bars and such like), female students being followed or having their bags snatched and children being bullied.

"Let him who desires peace, prepare for war!"

- Sun Tze

"Don't hit at all if it is honorably possible to avoid hitting; but never hit softly."

- *Theodore Roosevelt*

Lightning Source UK Ltd.
Milton Keynes UK
UKHW050631251121
394551UK00004B/397

9 781906 628741